AN OLD-FASHIONED

Christmas

Time-Life Books is a division of Time Life Inc.

TIME LIFE INC.
PRESIDENT AND CEO: George Artandi

TIME-LIFE CUSTOM PUBLISHING
Vice President and Publisher: Terry Newell
Vice President of Sales and Marketing: Neil Levin
Director of Special Sales: Liz Ziehl
Editor for Special Markets: Anna Burgard
Production Manager: Carolyn Clark
Quality Assurance Manager: James D. King

AN OLD-FASHIONED CHRISTMAS is an adaptation of the
AMERICAN COUNTRY series. AMERICAN COUNTRY was created
by Rebus, Inc. and published by Time-Life Books.

Adaptation Editor: Maryanne Bannon
New Craft Design: Chapelle Ltd.
New Craft Illustration: Pauline Locke

First printing. Printed in U.S.A.

Time-Life is a trademark of Time Warner Inc. U.S.A.

· ISBN: 0-7370-1123-8

The Library of Congress has cataloged the trade version of this title
as follows:

AN OLD-FASHIONED COUNTRY CHRISTMAS: a celebration of
the holiday season.
        p.   cm.
        Includes index.
        ISBN 0-7835-5283-1
        1. Christmas decorations.   2. Handicraft.
        3. Christmas Cookery
I. Time-Life Books.
TT900.C4035 1997
745.594'12--dc21   9728366
                    CIP

Books produced by Time-Life Custom Publishing are available at special bulk
discount for promotional and premium use. Custom adaptations can also be
created to meet your specific marketing goals. Call 1-800-323-5255.

AN OLD-FASHIONED

Christmas

DECORATIONS, CRAFTS, AND FESTIVE FOODS

ALEXANDRIA, VIRGINIA

INTRODUCTION

6

DECKING THE HALLS

8

SETTING THE CHRISTMAS TABLE

106

HOLIDAY ENTERTAINING

124

HOLIDAY BAKING

166

CRAFTING A COUNTRY CHRISTMAS

204

ACKNOWLEDGMENTS AND PHOTOGRAPHY CREDITS

INDEX

No other holiday evokes so many fond memories and so much eager anticipation as Christmas. No matter how busy our everyday lives, it is the season in which we pause to make time for celebrating the joys of family and friends. In the spirit of this most jubilant occasion, we decorate our homes, prepare special foods, and exchange tokens of love and good cheer. And while the spirit of Christmas is universal, we all celebrate the holiday in our own special style. Whether it is the choice of a bushy Scotch pine or elegant blue spruce as the family's Christmas tree, the setting up of grandpa's antique train set, the careful unwrapping of delicate heirloom ornaments, or the making of a favorite recipe passed from generation to generation, Christmas is not complete without family traditions.

Perhaps the reason that we are so fond of certain Christmas traditions is that many are deeply rooted in history. In most ancient, pre-Christian cultures throughout Europe and Britain, the winter solstice and the beginning of the new solar year were celebrated at the end of December. Festivals were attended, feasts were given, and gifts were exchanged. It was a festive as well as a spiritual celebration. Considered sacred, evergreens, which symbolize everlasting life, played an important ritualistic role in these festivities. Some greens, especially those that bear fruit in winter, were believed to have magical properties. Holly, for instance, was used for divining the future, while mistletoe was thought to cure infertility in animals. In Nordic cultures, mistletoe was a symbol of peace between enemies and love among friends. Kissing under the mistletoe is its modern echo. Our Christmas trees and garlands of evergreens are still symbolic of everlasting life, but have been adapted to Christian beliefs.

In this country, many of our holiday traditions emanated from our European ancestors and then developed a distinctive American style. Hessian soldiers fighting for the British in the Revolutionary War were the first to introduce Christmas trees to this country; at that time, however, they were small trees, placed on top of tables. It wasn't until the mid-nineteenth century that Christmas trees became popular, and then, because of our abundant forests, they were transformed into floor-to-ceiling wonders even in modest homes. The traditional goose of an English Christmas dinner gave way to the more patriotic choice of the native American turkey, and local foods like corn, cranberries, pumpkins, and wild rice provided the "fixings" for holiday meals. Perhaps the most dramatic American metamorphosis of European tradition was the transformation of the thin, austere Saint Nicholas, bishop of Myra, into the rotund, jolly Santa Claus with his flying reindeer and sleigh of gifts.

An Old-Fashioned Christmas celebrates these timeless yuletide traditions as they are lived today by families all across America. Generous homeowners take you on an exclusive tour of some of the most charmingly holiday-festooned country homes in the nation. From a one-time saddlery/tavern/country store and a Texas ranch to a Victorian "lady" and modern hacienda, you'll discover how others who love this season create old-fashioned holiday magic using personal flair and traditional accessories. *An Old-Fashioned Christmas* provides more than inspiration. It is a practical guide to creating your own very special Christmas celebration. We offer decorating tips and suggestions, provide the know-how to help you develop a personal holiday decor, and present delightful step-by-step projects for handcrafted accessories and gifts. And to go along with your family's favorite holiday dishes, we include a tasty collection of heritage recipes. Everything for the celebration is here—just add love for an old-fashioned Christmas.

Decking the Halls

Some Wonderful Ways to Decorate for a Country Christmas

The heart of Christmas is the home. And for many, before any cookies are baked or gifts wrapped, decorating the house is the first pleasure of the season. From selecting the tree and unpacking ornaments to setting up the Nativity figures, the traditions surrounding the holiday home are agreeably familiar and revitalizing. Some people enjoy it so much that they start decking the halls at Thanksgiving; and for those who like to make their own trimmings, preparations can commence even earlier in the year. Only after New Year's Day is the holiday finery reluctantly packed away.

Whether on the open range or a snowy Midwest farm, the essence of a country Christmas is found in friendly, homespun celebrations. At holiday time, many of the trimmings are chosen from family collections or with particular respect for the location and style of the house. Often, it is the simplest decorations that are the most effective—a garland of fresh pine boughs caught with ribbon bows, dried flowers used as tree ornaments, red-chili wreaths over the mantel, a candle in a window. Antique ornaments and feather trees, handcrafted Santas, Mexican candelabras, Nativity animals, and vintage toys also find a welcome place among the trimmings—all expressions of holiday good will.

A Festive Farmhouse

🍂

Familiar traditions make Christmas celebrations memorable for the owners of this 19th-century residence, originally part of a large Wisconsin farmstead. Every year the family host an open house, a Christmas Eve fondue party, and a treasure hunt for gifts.

An appreciation for tradition also influences the homeowners' choice of Christmas trimmings; long-time antiques collectors who particularly enjoy toys and folk art with an animal theme, they base their holiday decor on their favorite pieces. They try to include their collect-

The Wisconsin farmhouse at left was built in 1844 and still has its original clapboards and small "eyebrow" windows. At Christmas, the exterior is simply decorated with a wreath on the front door; a single candle glows in each window.

ibles in Christmas arrangements, and might add a jaunty bow to a carved piece or top a painting with a bit of greenery. Their holiday decorating extends not only throughout the house, but also to the bed-and-breakfast cottage they have re-modeled from an old smokehouse on the farm.

Appropriately, the tree is set up in the family room, the busiest room in the house, where much of the season's entertaining takes place. Here, the seven-foot balsam fir sparkles with tiny white lights and antique trimmings such as German glass kugels, clip-on candleholders,

Continued

The mid-19th-century toy rocking horse atop the old cupboard in the family room above wears a bow-bedecked wreath around its neck. A red-and-green Double Irish Chain quilt is hung behind at Christmas time.

wax angels, bead chains, cotton-batting ornaments, and a spun-glass angel at the top. Homemade popcorn garlands and ornaments made by the family's two children add a personal touch. Near the tree, flowering poinsettias—one placed in an old painted bucket, others in a buttocks basket—bring additional Christmas color to the room.

To take advantage of the large windows in the family room, ropes of greenery caught with red-ribbon bows are looped across the panes. On the windowsills, farm animals—pull-toy cows and horses and an old tin cow weathervane—are set out to "pasture." *Continued*

Red tree ornaments, poinsettias, and bows bring Christmas cheer to the family room at right. The table is set with 19th-century tea-leaf china.

Made with real fleece, pull-toy sheep like the circa 1880 German piece above were often displayed in crèches or under Christmas trees. This sheep is fitted with a bellows; when a string is pulled, the toy sounds a little bleat.

Holiday trimmings throughout the rest of the house are kept simple to harmonize with the understated furnishings. In the living room, for instance, the wing chair, camelback sofa, and early-18th-century Windsor chair are complemented by a few wreaths hung in the windows and by evergreen garlands on the sills. The mantelpiece is the setting for a flock of antique toy sheep, some of which were once used in elaborate Nativity scenes.

In this room, a small feather tree decorated with antique German glass ornaments stands in for a live evergreen. Still very popular, feather trees were introduced to America by German immigrants. The first artificial Christmas trees, they were traditionally made from dyed goose or

Continued

English and Irish samplers from the early 19th century, above, make an interesting backdrop for an old feather tree; the 19th-century molded and blown-glass ornaments are from Germany.

A toy collection, including a flock of antique sheep on the mantel, becomes part of the Christmas decorations in the living room at left.

Among the antique toys and folk-art pieces that the home-owners have been collecting for over twenty years are the sheep and horse set out on the 18th-century maple chest of drawers above. A bow lends seasonal color to the mid-19th-century oil painting.

turkey feathers wired to wooden dowels and were modeled after the sparse German *tannenbaum*, or silver fir. Feather trees had become common in America by the late 1800s, when a public outcry arose over the excessive cutting of ever-greens that occurred at Christmas time.

Traditional decorations can also be found in the master bedroom, where the pencil-post bed is decked with greenery and bright country textiles. While the Double Irish Chain quilt that hangs behind the bed is an antique, the quilts on the bed are contemporary pieces made by a rela-tive. Because one of the homeowners is a teach-er, the appliquéd Schoolhouse quilt has particu-lar meaning for the family. During the holidays,

Continued

Garlands and a wreath form a festive "canopy"
for the pencil-post tester bed at right.

Visitors staying in the smokehouse-turned-guest-cottage at right awake to a breakfast served on fine English china. A tabletop tree and toys nestled in greenery bring seasonal spirit to the room.

a favorite "portrait" of a cow is accented with a simple red and green bow.

The homeowners turned the old fieldstone smokehouse (above and preceding overleaf) into a bed-and-breakfast cottage soon after purchasing the farm, and enjoy taking the time to decorate it for guests each year. Here, a tabletop tree is set on an old quilt top and trimmed with popcorn garlands and miniature lights. Along the windowsill above the bed, greens form the backdrop for favorite pieces, including a small barn and rocking horse, a papier-mâché rabbit candy container, a large pull-toy horse, and a stuffed bear from England. Simple evergreen wreaths are placed on the exterior of the guest cottage, as well as on the doors of the barn.

The barn opposite is original to the 1844 farmstead. Completely renovated, it is now used by the homeowners for storing the antiques that they sell in a nearby shop.

HISTORY OF THE CHRISTMAS TREE

The tradition of the Christmas tree as we know it today is a relatively new one, first becoming widespread only in the 1800s. Yet it represents the influence of countless folk traditions and has roots extending to ancient times. Considered magical for their promise of life in the dead of winter, evergreens had particular significance in ancient pagan cultures, and by the Middle Ages had taken on meaning in the Christian religion. Greens were incorporated into medieval miracle plays based on Bible stories. During the Christmas season, a play honoring Adam and Eve was traditionally presented; an evergreen hung with apples, the fruit of knowledge, was the principal stage property. Villagers began imitating this "paradise" tree by decorating their own trees with apples, and the tradition continued long after the plays had disappeared.

Today's Christmas tree is probably the descendant of this paradise tree and of the German *lichtstock*—a wooden pyramid trimmed with evergreen sprigs, Nativity figures, and candles—that still appears in certain regions in Europe. At some point in time people began using the lichtstock candles on trees as well. One legend holds that Martin Luther introduced the lighted tree in the 1500s; supposedly, he was so taken

with the beauty of the night sky during a Christmas Eve walk that he brought home an evergreen for his children and decorated it with candles to simulate twinkling stars. A 19th-century painting of the scene helped to popularize the custom.

Christmas trees became increasingly common in Europe from the late 1700s onward and the tradition came to America with German settlers in the early 1800s. The tree really caught on in this country in 1850, when a newspaper illustration of Queen Victoria's lavishly ornamented tree at Windsor Castle was reprinted in America. Admirers of the royal family sought to imitate the scene in their own homes, decorating their trees with fruits, cookies, nuts, and paper flowers. It was not until the 1870s that commercially made ornaments were available in America.

Clockwise from upper left: a 1916 tinsel-decorated German Christmas tree; one of the earliest known depictions of an American Christmas tree, c. 1817; an English tree being topped with the Union Jack in 1876; an 1845 painting of Martin Luther and his candlelit tree; decorating the tree in the 1940s; Queen Victoria and Prince Albert display their tabletop tree at Windsor Castle in 1848; a tumbleweed tree in an Arizona schoolroom in 1907; a 1905 tree trimmed with candles and glass balls; German trees decorated with molded sugar-and-egg confections in the early 1800s.

A Warm Connecticut Christmas

Until the late 19th century, cookie cutters like the one above, shaped as Santa with his pack, were made from narrow strips of tin that were bent into fanciful forms and soldered to a tin backing; some five hundred different designs are known to exist.

Each room in this 1744 Connecticut farmhouse, decked out for the holidays, reflects a strong appreciation for colonial New England craftsmanship. Since restoring the house some thirty years ago, the owners have filled it with Connecticut and Massachusetts antiques that date from the late 1600s to about 1790. Many of the furnishings were made locally and represent some of the best workmanship of their time, and nearly every one has a tale of discovery associated with it.

At Christmas time, the decorations and preparations also reveal a fascination with history. In each room, the flicker of candlelight contributes to the sense of time gone by. All of the candles are hand-dipped by one of the homeowners, who has taught country crafts such as candlemaking at the farm. "I prefer the colors I am able to achieve by dipping to those of candles that can be found in the stores," she says.

To maintain the early look of the house, the various holiday trimmings are intentionally kept simple but cheerful. "The first colonists did not decorate at Christmas," the owner explains, "but they did use a lot of color in their homes." For a homespun, natural look, fragrant garlands of pine embellished with little more than a few apples, pinecones, or dried pomegranates are favored.

All of the greens—holly, boxwood, white

Continued

Tiny tree lights and hand-dipped candles create soft lighting in this farmhouse parlor at Christmas. Carefully chosen antiques include the country Queen Anne desk from Connecticut, left. The fireplace lintel above was carved when a prosperous farmer, Colonel Samuel Clark, owned the house.

Simple touches of greenery add holiday spirit to the old kitchen—now used as a living room. Restored to working order by the owners, the large fireplace had been covered over with boards and bricks. The unusual 17th-century chair in the foreground, a prized piece, has an angel-and-heart design carved into its crest, and is thought to have been made as a wedding gift for its original owner, Metta Hauschildt.

pine, laurel leaves, as well as a fir tree—come from the farm. Sparkling with tiny white lights, the handsome tree is set up in the parlor and decorated with baby's-breath and achillea (some of which is dyed a rosy color), picked from the homeowners' garden, and with home-baked ginger-cookie hearts shaped with an old tin cookie cutter. "Gathering greenery and making the decorations are half the joy of Christmas," says one owner. Also welcome are decorations made by friends, such as the small ivy topiary—trained over a chicken-wire base—that are placed on the hearth in the old kitchen (preceding overleaf).

Holiday trimmings also appear in the master bedroom, where—played off against the colors of the painted woodwork and antique textiles—they create a feeling of warmth that offsets the chill New England light. Baskets of poinsettias set on a bench provide Christmas color at the foot of the bed. And on a drop-leaf table by the windows, Japanese andromeda, white pine, and black alder twigs with bright red berries make a simple but effective arrangement.

Federal-period antiques in the master bedroom include the field bed at left and the mirror above, a Massachusetts piece distinguished by a gold frame and reverse painting on glass. The graceful Queen Anne drop-leaf table, from Connecticut, has been in the family since the 1700s.

A Christmas Showcase

🌿

This brick and fieldstone Pennsylvania farmhouse, built in two parts during the 18th century, is a showcase for the present owners' antiques and Christmas decorations. Because one family member's birthday falls in December, the holidays have become a dual celebration that continues to grow in scope.

The owners search for new Christmas decorating ideas throughout the year and begin to ready the house for the yuletide season just after Thanksgiving. Several trees are set up, and the entire house is filled with Santas and

The family that live in the historic Pennsylvania house at left are descendants of the original Quaker owners. The brick portion was built in 1705 and the field-stone addition dates from 1783.

bearded gnomes known as Belsnickels (an extensive collection of Christmas figures, both old and new, numbers over three hundred). "Friends started giving me Santas and ornaments for my birthday," explains one homeowner, "and it all just evolved from there."

Santas, however, are only the beginning; the family also decorate with imaginative arrangements of antiques, grouping sleds and baby carriages under the various trees and placing toys and folk-art pieces on mantels and windowsills. Food also plays a role: pretzels, dried fruits, and

Continued

31

Dominated by the original walk-in fireplace, the family room at right is particularly inviting at holiday time. Bottle brush trees from the 1920s and vintage Santas adorn the mantel.

homemade cookies are fashioned into ornaments and garlands.

As a result, each room has its own warm character. Located in the late-18th-century stone section of the house, the family room (preceding overleaf) is decorated informally to enhance its cozy atmosphere. Here, the tree is trimmed especially to appeal to children. This entails using a variety of homemade edible ornaments—strings of dark and golden raisins, gin-

gerbread cookies, sand tarts, popcorn garlands, and pretzel rings. While beeswax candles are fastened to the branches, the tapers are not actually lit; instead, the homeowners use tiny white lights to simulate the glow of candlelight.

The tree in the dining room at right is decorated more formally, and with a Victorian flair. Trimming a tree with flags was particularly popular in the late 19th century, and the tradition is recalled here with American flags found in a

Continued

Dried flowers, including cockscomb and Queen Anne's lace, as well as flags (probably made in the 1940s) and candles, decorate the distinctive dining room tree above and at right. The doll carriage and "belly" sled underneath date from the 1860s.

First used around 1878, counterweight candleholders, or candle bobs, like the 1890s examples above, were designed to hang on tree branches. The bodies of the angel and Santa are weighted to keep the candles upright.

A kissing ball—*a popular Christmas decoration in Victorian times—hangs from the chandelier in the breakfast room at right. Homemade from dried mistletoe, evergreens, and flowers, it is saved and used year after year.*

summer house many years ago. The homeowners have also added flowers picked from their own garden earlier in the year and then dried: fuzzy cockscomb, yellow yarrow, delicate clusters of Queen Anne's lace, starflowers, lavender, roses, and salvia. The other ornaments include dried pomegranates strung on red cord, tin icicles, and candle bobs.

The breakfast room at left is part of a wing added to the house in 1970. This informal dining area is appropriately decorated with Christmas edibles. Gingerbread men are lined up along a swing-up bar grate, which is also trimmed with a chain of dried apple slices set off by greenery. In a window, more apple slices are gathered with twine into miniature wreaths, while little bundles of two or three cinnamon sticks are tied up with red yarn. The chain is made from apples and filberts strung on a wire and finished off with a pretty plaid bow. *Continued*

Set atop a 19th-century blanket chest, the breakfast room tree above features ornaments relating to the goat, the family "mascot." The ceramic Santa Claus mugs displayed beneath the tree date from the 1930s.

Also in the breakfast room is the "goat tree." Because one of the owners grew up on a horse farm where goats were kept to calm the skittish thoroughbreds, the goat has been adopted as a whimsical family mascot. Each year, a small tabletop tree is decorated with 19th-century tin, wooden, and ceramic toy goats from their collection, and with related items such as bundles of hay bound with string and little fences homemade from matchsticks. The tiny wreath atop the tree even features a small, wooden goat's head inside it.

Christmas spirit is also extended to the bedrooms. In the guest room above and at right, a group of wooden Santa figures find a place on the mantelpiece, while a 19th-century rocking horse and a contemporary carved Santa stand by the hearth. Hanging from the feather tree in the window are wooden Noah's ark animals. And on the Victorian dressing table, the homeowners have set up a festive holiday "tea party," complete with miniature furniture, stuffed bears, a doll's tea set—and even a tiny feather tree centerpiece.

Stockings made from old quilt fragments are hung by the chimney with care in the guest room above.
The warm country feeling in the room is enhanced by the collection of well-loved antique toys at right,
including a Victorian-era stuffed bear and 1920s pull-toy dog.

The egg-shaped Santa above, known as a roly-poly, was made as a toy; when it is tipped over, it pops right back up. The piece was produced around 1910 by the Schoenhut toy factory of Philadelphia, which manufactured many different roly-poly Santas.

It's Christmas, Naturally!

Begin planning your natural Christmas in July. When November arrives, you'll be glad you took advantage of nature's generosity.

◆ Press small flowers, petals, and leaves between the pages of heavy books. Use a dab of white glue to add red and white flowers and green leaves to gift tags and Christmas cards.

◆ Scour the beach for interesting shells that can later be used to make simple ornaments. Spray shells with metallic or other color paint, hot-glue a wire hanger, and tie with a bow made from $1/8$-inch-wide ribbon.

Many of the things that are used for beautiful natural decorations can be found right in the aisles of the local grocery.

◆ Wire cinnamon sticks together in bunches and tie with red gingham ribbon or raffia. Wire or hot-glue these to plain napkin rings, or attach them to a wreath or garland.

◆ Fresh herbs are now available year round packaged in small plastic bags in the produce area of most better markets. Buy whatever looks freshest and add sprigs to wreaths, swags, and garlands, Not only do the varied leaves add texture to your decorations, but they emit a subtle scent as well.

◆ Cheerful citrus colors add to the festiveness of the season. Try a variation on the pomander theme: Stud grapefruits with cloves, as well as the traditional oranges, lemons, and limes. Kumquats, which look like tiny oval oranges, are easy to string into garlands, but be sure to use under-ripe ones as they perish quickly.

◆ Dried fruits can be used alone or as colorful additions for garlands and wreaths. You can dry citrus fruits, apples, and pears in an oven set at 125° to 150°F. Cut the fruit into slices about $1/4$ inch thick. Lay them in a single layer on a wire rack and place in the oven. Turn the fruits every 20 minutes. Keep in the oven $1^1/_2$ to 2 hours. The warm fruit may not seem completely dry; set in an open, dry area to cool and dry further.

◆ For a classic Christmas garland, use a sharp needle and double-length of sewing thread to string cranberries and popcorn. If you use pre-popped popcorn, be sure to get the plain unbuttered variety.

◆ The graceful shape of the pear and its subtle coloration add a note of sophistication to holiday compositions. Select pears that are not quite ripe—they will last about a week. Be careful; they bruise easily.

◆ Pomegranates range in color from red to pink-blushed yellow. They will last all season and take on a more interesting texture as they air-dry.

◆ If you live in a very cold climate, it's best not to use fresh fruits on outside decorations such as door wreaths. Fortunately, luscious-looking faux fruits are widely available in craft stores.

◆ To make a fruit cone, use an inverted Styrofoam™ cone for the base. Impale fruits at various angles, using skewers for the large ones and toothpicks for the smaller ones. Insert the skewered fruit into the cone and fill in gaps with boxwood sprigs.

A trip to a crafts store and/or floral supplier can provide a treasure trove of materials and ideas for your decorating projects.

◆ Holly and ivy, fresh or faux? Once cut, holly and ivy are more perishable than other greens. Ivy wilts after a day or two, especially near a heating source, and the leaves and berries of holly begin to fall off even if it's kept in water. Cut holly just before the Christmas party and replace with fresh as the holiday season progresses. Don't be afraid to use artificial holly and ivy. The quality of artificial greens, flowers, and berries is so superior to what it once was that it really pays to invest in quality "silks" that can be used year after year. Best of all, they look fabulous and don't lose their leaves.

◆ When making wreaths, swags, and garlands, begin with a base of artificial greens. They are much easier to work with than fresh, are fuller and more pliable, and last for many seasons. Add fresh herbs and freshly cut greens for fragrance, and fruits, nuts, and berries for a lushly rich look. At the end of the holidays, remove any perishable items and store the faux greens until next Christmas.

◆ Purchase several gauges of florist's wire to have on hand during the holiday decorating season. The lighter weight, #22, comes on a small spool and is perfect for wiring small clusters of herbs or berries to wreaths, while the heavier wire, #16, will firmly hold fruit, large nuts, and large pine cones. Florist's tape can be used to wrap sprigs of greens, flowers, or herbs together.

◆ Sheet moss, also available by the bag, is ideal for a variety of decorating uses from creating topiaries and tabletop trees to disguising the soil in flowerpots.

I n central Texas, the winters are mild. "Even at Christmas time," says one of the owners of this 1870s farmhouse, "I can usually cut flowers in the garden for centerpieces, and we can still enjoy dining on the back porch—our favorite place to eat."

Used as a weekend home by a Houston couple and their three daughters, the house is situated on a 136-acre expanse of farmland. With its simple lines, it is typical of many farmhouses in central Texas built by German immigrants in the second half of the 19th century. The paneled and painted rooms are showcases for the couple's collection of Texas furnishings, also crafted by the German settlers; using hand tools and local woods such as longleaf pine and cypress, the

Continued

A ten-foot table, above, is used for outdoor family dining about ten months out of the year. Decoys, cedar boughs, pinecones, and fruit make up the Christmas centerpiece.

Built by German settlers in the 1870s, this Texas farmhouse features a breezy front porch, opposite, with gingerbread trim typical of the period and region. A simple wreath decorates the door at holiday time.

immigrants created vernacular furniture in the Biedermeier style then popular in their homeland. Because the furniture was made only from around 1840 to 1870, it is quite rare and is eagerly sought after today.

Complementing the furniture are the family's collections of antique toys and stars, which are continually rearranged throughout the house and which look particularly effective at Christmas. Red-and-white quilts and embroidered pillow shams also provide bright notes of color in keeping with the season. "I've never had the couches upholstered, the owner says, "because it's much more interesting to use different quilts as coverings instead."

Beginning in November, the women in the family cut grapevines in the yard and twine them into wreaths to hang in the house or to give as gifts. As the holiday approaches, they gather native cedar and yaupon (a type of holly with shiny green leaves and red berries) from the property and use the cuttings to decorate tables and mantelpieces. "I like to keep the decorations as they might have been when the original

Continued

In the living room, candies are clustered in bowls, above, while vine wreaths hang by the fireplace at right; on the mantle is an embroidered shelf trimming of the type used in pantries in 19th-century German-American households. The message conveys the blessing "Compassion and Purity."

settlers lived here," says one of the homeowners.

The small trees that are set up in the bedrooms have been cut to thin out the grove of cedars in the yard. Instead of using conventional ornaments on these unique Christmas trees, the owners opt for toys and textiles. On one, miniature dustpans, buckets, and chairs appear; another is trimmed with children's clothing and a small patchwork Christmas stocking. Because the family collections include antique cookie cutters, the annual round of Christmas baking usually produces several batches of cookie ornaments as well. Such improvised decorations only add to the old-fashioned warmth of the house.

In the bedroom opposite, a mantel decked with holiday greenery becomes a festive showcase
for the homeowners' collections of 19th-century papier-mâché horses and redware apple banks,
which were made from about 1700 to the mid-1800s.

Christmas Stockings

The custom of hanging stockings by the fireplace on Christmas Eve can be traced to a Saint Nicholas legend. To help an impoverished nobleman provide dowries for his daughters, the generous Saint Nick threw gold coins down the chimney. The coins magically landed in stockings hung by the fire to dry. In America, those hoping for a sampling of Saint Nick's beneficence began hanging stockings—either from the mantel, staircase, or tree—in the early 1800s.

The first stockings were no more than or-

Hung by the chimney with care, the vintage stockings at left range from simple everyday hose to the fancy printed types popular from the 1890s to the 1930s. The patchwork stocking is homemade from flannel and twill scraps. The three brick-patterned stockings bear holiday sayings, including a quote from Clement Moore's "A Visit from St. Nicholas."

dinary booties and socks borrowed for holiday service. Homemakers might also decorate such stockings with embroidery or make more elaborate ones from cloth remnants. In the late 1800s, the first commercially made Christmas stockings became available. Most featured scenes printed on thin cotton or linen and were sold either already assembled or as patterns to be cut and sewn at home. The most popular images included Santa descending a brick chimney, an "x-ray" view of a stocking's contents, or scenes of stockings hung by the fire.

Christmas Past

The owners of this late-19th-century house believe in preserving the past. Abandoning city life in the 1970s, they purchased a neglected farmstead at auction and renovated and enlarged the old house themselves. Their appreciation of history extends not only to the carefully chosen furnishings that now fill the house, but also to their Christmas decorations, which include toys, feather trees, and a collection of antique ornaments.

To show off their favorite ornaments—kugels, wax angels, printed paper "scraps," and chains

Continued

Crafted by a family member, the feather tree above is designed with branches on only two sides so that it can be easily placed against a window or wall. The brass wreath is made from animal, tree, sleigh, and angel shapes cast from old candy molds.

On the family room mantelpiece at left, Santas handcrafted by a friend appear to tend German toy sheep. The vine wreaths are homemade.

51

of colorful glass beads made in 19th-century Germany and Czechoslovakia—the homeowners specifically choose a balsam tree for its short needles and long, well-spaced branches. "We used to cut down our own tree every year and always looked for one with an old bird's nest in it," recalls one family member. "Now we buy a tree and put a nest in it ourselves."

Favoring natural materials and fresh greenery, the family also craft many of their decorations, which include grapevine wreaths for the family room (preceding overleaf). These might be trimmed with antique toys, spun-cotton fruits, pinecones, and fresh cedar sprigs. Hand-

made as well are a number of feather trees, crafted from dyed goose feathers and displayed throughout the house. Such holiday finery may even be found in the sewing room, where an antique feather tree twinkles with bead chains; gathered like presents around its base are a roly-poly Santa, antique dolls, and one of the many miniature sewing machines in the homeowners' collection.

Cooking is also an important part of the family's holiday celebration, and many of their kitchen collectibles, including vintage cookie cutters, are pressed into service for Christmas baking. In the cozy kitchen are simple decorations such

Continued

During the 19th and early 20th centuries, many pincushions were designed to be ornamental and were often given as gifts. Cushions like the beaded velvet piece, top, which may have been made by American Indians for trade in the early 1900s, and the Victorian-era boot, bottom, are now popular collectibles.

In addition to sewing machines, lace—stored on old bobbins in the sewing room opposite—and pincushions, including the beaded pieces from the 1890s on the windowsill above, are collected by the homeowners. The framed work is a German house blessing spelled out in pins.

Fresh greenery, rolling pins and cutting boards, and a pinecone wreath studded with spun-cotton fruits make a charming Christmas still life in a corner of the kitchen.

as greenery and pinecone wreaths; here, evergreen sprays sprout from an old chicken scale and a few bright red apples nest in a bed of pine. Like the trimmings in the rest of the house, these seasonal touches have an informal, comfortable character. "We don't consciously follow any one holiday decorating scheme," say the owners. "We've always collected old things and just enjoy using what we have."

Shiny apples and a few sprigs of pine bring yuletide cheer to this country kitchen; vintage utensils still come in handy for holiday baking.

A Collector's Christmas

N ew and vintage folk art—cleverly arranged by an enthusiastic collector—distinguishes the Christmas decor in this Pennsylvania home. Built in the mid-18th century, the historic structure has housed a saddlery, a tavern, and several general stores over the years. Part of the building is still used as a country store by the present owners; instead of seed and overalls, however, the shopkeepers now purvey folk art pieces, as well as antique and reproduction country furnishings.

The living quarters of the building have been carefully renovated to provide an appropriate backdrop for the family's antiques and collections. Christmas decorating starts the day after Thanksgiving in the keeping room, a combination kitchen and family room (left and overleaf) that the homeowners created by removing a partition. "Since we've been here ten years, I pretty much know the areas I want to decorate," says one family member, "but I like to change the materials and look each year." Because it is a large space, a number of small groupings are planned throughout the room; many include contemporary folk-art decorations from the owners' store.

The setup shown here features Santa figures parading across the kitchen island (cotton batting provides a snowy ground beneath them).

Continued

Fragrant and pretty, fresh greens—including fir, juniper, holly, and delicate sprigs of cedar—are tucked here and there in the keeping room, left.

57

The ceiling-high tree in the keeping room is decorated with contemporary folk-art ornaments; whimsical trinkets also find a place on the boughs. Branches of pine and red-berried holly are arranged on tables and windowsills. Dried pomegranates nest in greenery atop the window sashes.

The mantelpiece across the room has become a Christmas homestead, complete with an antique miniature log cabin, farm animals, and a tiny woodpile. The homeowners also take advantage of the space offered by the deep-set windows in the room, varying the arrangements on each sill. On one, a few pieces of redware crockery are joined by some berry-sprigged branches to make a casual but striking still life, while on the other, handcrafted Santas and an assortment of farm animal figures appear to have gathered for their own celebration.

The focal point of the room, however, is the nearly ten-foot-tall tree. The ornaments, which are all contemporary pieces, are a colorful mix of traditional glass balls, Santas, and gingerbread men, as well as miniature baskets, tin quilt motifs, cardboard folk-art figures, and even a scherenschnitt Noah's ark; a smiling rag-doll angel is placed at the top. To emphasize the country look of the tree even more, the base has been turned into a whimsical farmyard scene where toy sheep, pigs, and a cow graze together on a bed of hay. *Continued*

The collection of contemporary handcrafted Santas above includes a tall, brown-suited figure made from clay and a stuffed-cotton piece emerging from a wooden "brick" chimney. The small cedar tree is decked with lamb's-wool sheep, clay stars and hearts, tin stars, and white tallow berries.

The cheerful red-and-green color scheme of the guest room at right provides the perfect backdrop for Christmas decorations. The country wreath is made from rose hips.

A small Fraser fir suits the cozy bedroom above. The figure of the little girl is a reproduction of a dummy board.

In contrast to the first-floor keeping room, the upstairs bedrooms are decorated very simply. In a guest room (preceding overleaf), a red-and-white quilt is brought out each year to provide Christmas color. Princess pine roping entwined with popcorn frames the peg rack and door, and sugar-cookie men hang from the garland.

In another bedroom, above and opposite, the setting features a small fir tree trimmed with red ribbon bows, dried apple slices, cinnamon hearts, rose hips, and shortbread cookies. Lace collars and sprigs of holly tucked into the three-tiered wall basket over the bed add an especially festive note.

Tucking a few evergreen boughs and some branches of holly around a collection of bandboxes was all it took to create the striking Christmas vignette atop the wardrobe opposite. An antique tin monkey jumping jack hangs from the latch. The Noah's ark is a contemporary work.

Santa Figures

Dating to the late 19th century, the figures at right are gift-bearers derived from Saint Nicholas, a 4th-century bishop (shown with staff and miter at center). Not all are kindly: those carrying switches, like the German Knecht Rupprecht in the green cloak (far right), are alter egos of the saint, meant to frighten bad children. The figure dressed in red has dropped a naughty child into his pack.

The jolly, red-suited Santa Claus of modern Christmas lore is a composite of many folk figures—some benevolent and others surprisingly stern and forbidding. Over the years, the gift-bearer in his various incarnations has been reproduced in a number of forms, including a wide range of figures, some of which were used as ornaments, toys, and candy containers.

Many Santa pieces were made by German toymakers between 1860 and World War II, but some were also produced in 20th-century America and Japan. Figures ranging in height from a few inches to several feet can be found in chalkware, papier-mâché, wood, cardboard, or composition, and might be decorated with paint, fabric, fur, mica glitter, or cotton batting.

Most Santa characters are related to Saint

Continued

The composition and papier-mâché Belsnickels opposite were made in Germany and range in size from 2½ to 24 inches. The larger figures are the scarcest.

Crafted mainly in Germany, the figures above depict Santa as the kindly present-bearer we imagine him as today. The jack-in-the-box is a rare and desirable piece.

Nicholas, a legendary bishop who lived in Asia Minor in the 4th century. Known for his generous deeds in life, Nicholas was immortalized as the patron saint of children, who brought them gifts on December 5, the eve of his feast day. The charitable Nicholas was supposedly accompanied by a grotesque helper who punished the bad with coal and switches. This alter ego was variously known as Knecht Rupprecht (Servant Ruppert), Ru Klas (Rough Nicholas), or Pelz-Nikolaus (Fur-clad Nicholas), among other personas. Pelz-Nikolaus emigrated to America with German settlers and became known as Belsnickel. Today Belsnickel figures made in Germany between the 1870s and 1920 (and occasionally in America) are particularly popular

with Santa collectors. These gnomish, bearded figures carry evergreen sprigs or switches in their arms and are dressed in hooded cloaks.

With the Protestant Reformation in the 16th century, which forbade worship of saints, Nicholas took on a secular aspect: in England he became Father Christmas, for example, and in Germany, Weihnachtsmann (Christmas man). It is this secular Nicholas that is the basis for to-day's Santa, who, as Sinterklaas, came to America with the Dutch in 1624. Several literary works, including Clement Moore's 1822 poem "A Visit from St. Nicholas," helped transform the thin European saint into the rotund elf in fur-trimmed suit and cap we now envision as Santa Claus.

When Benjamin Stauffer, a successful physician, built this distinctive red-brick house in rural Pennsylvania in 1848, he probably hoped to impress his neighbors. But while the elegant design of the front door and roof cornice gave his home the look of an imposing town house, the rooms inside, with their high ceilings, simple moldings, and painted trim, were still in keeping with the unaffected feeling of a country setting.

In restoring the house, the present owners have intentionally preserved the mix of refinement and small-town Pennsylvania charm that Dr. Stauffer built in. The couple have furnished the house with country antiques—painted cupboards, Windsor chairs, and walnut tables—

Continued

Balsam garlands deck the front hall staircase above. The 1800s tall clock was made by Emanuel Meily, a Pennsylvania weaver who also excelled at cabinetmaking.

Garlands and a wreath decorate the Greek Revival doorway of the Pennsylvania farmhouse opposite.

The old summer kitchen at right now serves as a casual living room. The small tree in the window is decorated with fraktur-inspired ornaments and soft-sculpture heart-and-hands.

The heart-and-hand motif has appeared in American folk art since the 18th century. Symbolizing love and loyalty, it is seen often in Pennsylvania-German decoration. This contemporary heart-and-hand was stitched as a tree ornament.

that were made in the surrounding area. They also collect the work of contemporary craftspeople who carve and paint pieces in traditional Pennsylvania folk-art styles.

During the Christmas season, some of those pieces, such as handmade tree ornaments and carved crèche figures, are welcome additions to the trimmings. And there are always a few new decorations to surprise relatives when they return for the holiday. The small window tree in the living room (preceding overleaf), as well as the large tree in the dining room (see pages 126-127), for example, are decorated with contemporary fraktur ornaments, inspired by the illustrated manuscripts of the Pennsylvania Germans. *Continued*

The folk-art rooster in the Christmas vignette above recalls the work of William Schimmel,

a 19th-century Pennsylvania carver.

Topped by pine sprigs, the frames on the folk-art prints in the living room at left were crafted and grain-painted by the homeowners. The three-story dollhouse boasts its own tiny Christmas tree behind the miniature picket fence, as well as a pair of delightfully oversized stockings.

73

Taufshein, or baptismal records, like the framed example above, were traditionally kept by Pennsylvania-German families. The Nativity figures displayed below the work were carved and painted by a contemporary craftsman.

Caught up in the spirit of Christmas, the family always embrace the season's traditions wholeheartedly. Every niche and window ledge holds a reminder of the holiday. Greens and ribbons deck picture frames and mirrors. Even in the bedrooms, clusters of folk-art toys and greenery create a sense of nostalgic charm.

"Celebration is important and decorating is part of the enchantment, but it doesn't just happen," says one owner. "Preparations can be exhausting—particularly when it's two a.m. and the tree lights don't work—but it's worth it," she adds. "It's a gift to your family and friends."

Folk-art toys sporting bright red ribbons add Christmas cheer to the bedroom at right.

CARDS BY LOUIS PRANG

The custom of exchanging Christmas cards was already established by the time Louis Prang produced his first cards in the early 1870s. But it was the German-immigrant printer who was responsible for bringing fine-art standards to this commercial commodity and for popularizing greeting cards in America.

Prang arrived in this country in 1850 at age twenty-six. In 1860, he opened his own chromolithography shop, L. Prang & Co., near Boston, where he specialized in quality art reproductions, maps, and trade cards. After an associate suggested that his floral-decorated business cards would also make appealing Christmas greetings, Prang printed his first cards for the English market in 1874. Their immediate acceptance led Prang to sell his cards the next year in America, where only European cards had been available.

Early Prang cards measured about 2 by 3½ inches and were printed with an image and a brief message on one side. During the next twenty years, his cards increased in size to 7 by 10 inches, carried longer verse, and were printed on both sides. Common motifs included flowers, birds, winter scenes, and angels.

Regardless of size or subject, all of Prang's cards displayed the technical excellence he demanded. They were printed using from eight to twenty color plates, and often featured black or red backgrounds to enhance the

designs. While Prang deemed lace, mechanical tricks, and other novelties vulgar, he did permit silk fringe and tassels.

To ensure the quality of his cards, Prang initiated an annual Christmas card design competition in 1880. Judged by leading artists, architects, and designers, the prestigious contest eventually offered prizes of up to $2,000. Not only did Prang publish cards with winning works by such well-known contemporary artists as Thomas Moran and Elihu Vedder, he used losing entries, too.

Although Prang's cards were costlier than his competitors'—they were priced up to $1—they were more popular; the company printed nearly five million cards annually. By the late 1800s, however, inexpensive European Christmas postcards had eroded Prang's business. Rather than lower his prices by lowering his standards, he turned his presses to educational book printing in 1897.

The Christmas cards pictured on these two pages are examples of the exquisitely lithographed greetings produced by the printer Louis Prang, often called the father of the American Christmas card. The artwork for all of these cards was taken from winning entries in the Christmas card design competitions Prang held between 1880 and 1884. These high-profile contests were meant to increase both the popularity of the Christmas card and the public's appreciation of fine art.

Holiday
Artistry

Simple garlands, handmade
Santas, and a collection of
feather trees decorate the
family room, right. A twig
fence surrounds the group
of trees on the chest.
Such fences were popular
under-the-tree decorations
beginning in the late 1800s
and usually enclosed a
village, Nativity, or
farm scene.

The owners of this 1860s Wisconsin farmhouse blend the furnishings and Christmas collectibles they have acquired over time with newly crafted ornaments for an original holiday decor. One of the homeowners is an artist and dollmaker who spends several months each year preparing for a local Christmas crafts fair; her own Santas and folk figures, as well as other pieces made by friends, have particular personal meaning.

Rather than concentrating their efforts in any one room, the family enjoy decorating the entire house, favoring vignettes of antique toys or single folk-art pieces trimmed with a bit of greenery. The simplicity of the decorations—a garland strung over a window or from a beam—is especially well suited to the homey look of the old house, and the arrangements can be easily changed according to the family's whims.

Continued

An angel doll, above, crafted by one of the homeowners, sits comfortably inside a distinctive wreath made of cedar, pinecones, cinnamon sticks, and berries. Completing this family room scene are a selection of pieces collected over the years: a vintage pencil box, a tin car from the 1920s, and a mechanical bank.

Decorated with winter scenes, tins once used to package cookies, candies, and other Christmas treats make cheerful decorations long after their edible contents have disappeared. The square box, top, is an English biscuit tin; the round tin, bottom, made in America around the 1950s, held fruitcake.

The antique furnishings, gathered over the years from local shops or discovered at flea markets, also become a natural part of the Christmas decorating scheme. In the family room, for example, an old log sled and a newspaper delivery wagon serve as the settings for homemade holiday treats and a tea party for two handcrafted bears.

Most arrangements incorporate feather trees from the family's extensive collection, which includes antiques and reproductions in many sizes. They appear throughout the house, atop tables and chests or clustered on windowsills.

Some of the feather trees are trimmed with simple red berry ornaments—a berry or candleholder at the tip of each branch was the German custom—while others are left plain. The largest of the feather trees displayed in the family room is decorated with cherry-shaped candies strung on wires, papier-mâché stars, and anise-flavored candy rings.

Another feather tree, an antique, is set on a butcher block to provide Christmas cheer in a corner of the kitchen, opposite. Arranged as "gifts" around its base and on the floor is a prized collection of vintage food tins. A second

Continued

Above, the pine refectory table in the kitchen is set with an antique tea-leaf ironstone coffeepot and the family's heirloom Christmas china—a red-and-green floral pattern by Johnson Brothers, an English porcelain firm.

A turn-of-the-century addition to the 1860s house, the kitchen is decorated for the yuletide season. Opposite, an antique feather tree strung with garlands of tiny stars sits atop a butcherblock surrounded by a collection of vintage food tins.

Many childhood treasures have been used to decorate the upstairs hallway at right for the holidays. Among the children's books displayed on the log beam is one about Saint Nicholas.

grouping of tins set out on a dry sink is trimmed with evergreen sprigs, candy canes, and pinecones. Above the sink hang a trio of tiny straw wreaths dressed up for Christmas.

Even out-of-the-way spaces like the upstairs hallway above get special attention. Here, looking as though it would be the perfect spot for a child to await Santa's arrival, a small rocking bed, covered with a feather ticking and a Log Cabin quilt, is tucked into the corner. A pine garland hangs from the beam above the bed, as do handmade stockings sewn from a crazy patchwork of velvet and antique lace remnants. A collection of toys, including dolls and trains, as well as children's books, is lined up along the top of the beam, and an old chalkboard mounted on the wall proclaims the family's good wishes for the holiday season.

Fast and Festive Decorating Ideas

You don't have to spend a lot of time or money to create beautiful holiday decorations. There are many common objects that with a little dressing up are perfect as Christmas decorations.

◆ Accent your hallway staircase with an unusual garland. Instead of decking it with greenery, fashion a graceful garland from pretty fabric tied with wide wire-edged ribbon bows, or tie green and red bandannas together and drape them along the banister.

◆ Embellish a plain sisal doormat by using stencils and spray paint to decorate with a holiday design.

◆ Sew a few red and green rag rugs together end to end, alternating the colors, to create a holiday floor runner for a hallway.

◆ Use Christmas-theme gift bags sold at stationery stores to cover the plain plastic pots in which Christmas plants and poinsettias come. Or, fold over the top edge of a brown grocery bag to the height of the pot. Hang a crocheted doily over one edge. Place the plant inside.

◆ For an instant holiday look for your sofa and chairs, "wrap" each throw pillow with wide colorful ribbon as you would a gift package and tie a bow on top.

◆ For candleholders with old-fashioned appeal, hot-glue wrapped peppermint candies or cinnamon sticks to the outside of old glasses, then tie with a bright ribbon.

◆ Place votive candles on a plate or bowl filled with coarse salt for "candles in the snow."

◆ Place cup hooks on the upper outer edges of a window. Make a swag using your favorite ornaments and linked chain found in hardware stores. Drape the chain on the hooks, letting it dip in the middle and fall halfway down each side of the window. Hang ornaments on the chain until it is covered. You can also tie twine or ribbon from the hooks and hang old or mismatched mittens along the twine using painted clothespins.

◆ Create a white Christmas. Tape paper doilies to windows. Spray with artificial snow and remove the doilies.

◆ Hot-glue small pine cones, berries, and red, green, or gold buttons to a piece of wide ribbon to make a festive tieback for draperies. Let the excess ribbon dangle from a knot and cut the ends of the ribbon on an angle. Or, gather a bunch of jingle bells on a decorative cord and tie around a drapery panel as a tieback.

◆ Festoon a chandelier or candelabrum by swagging ribbon among the arms. Tie a bow or hang an ornament on each arm.

Holiday
Elegance

The sunny garden room at right, overlooking a sweeping valley, is decorated with an abundance of natural greenery. "Each year we add more and more," says a family member, who gathered the pine boughs from the property.

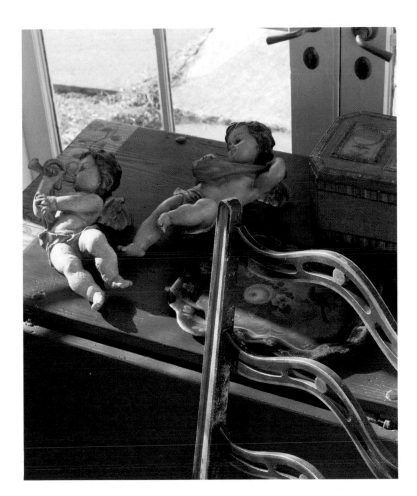

Every year, this hillside home in the Berkshire Mountains of Massachusetts becomes the setting for a joyous country Christmas with decorations that are simple yet elegant.

In one of two sunny garden rooms, for example, the French doors are effectively crowned with swags of laurel, hemlock, and spruce, and are trimmed with lush pinecone-studded evergreen wreaths. The focal point of the decorations, however, is the dramatic tree, often as tall as fourteen feet, placed in the curve of the elegant living room staircase (overleaf), where it rises all the way to the second floor landing. The majestic tree is decorated generously, and all sorts of ornaments, from glass balls to a multitude of hearts—crafted in glass, wood, metal, and paper—find a place on the branches. "We

Continued

Collected on the homeowners' travels, the putti above, set on an 18th-century Swedish table in the garden room, are contemporary Italian reproductions made of polychrome wood. Such celestial figures were common in Renaissance art, and often appeared in European Nativity scenes in the 1700s.

Made of wood and decorated with metallic paints, the small winged cherub face above—a copy of an 18th-century Spanish piece—is from Barcelona.

*Garlands draped along
the curving banister
frame the fourteen-foot
tree in the living
room at left.*

On the living room table at right, a poinsettia in full blossom calls attention to a collection of silver, porcelain, and cloisonné boxes. Nearby, a papier-mâché reindeer peeks from behind a comfortable armchair.

have been collecting ornaments for more than forty years and buy them everywhere, looking for all periods and types," say the homeowners. "Friends also give them to us each year."

Found throughout the living room are surprising, original seasonal touches. A pressed-glass compote filled with small red glass balls that resemble bunches of grapes, for example, makes an unusual and striking accessory on an antique candlestand, while papier-mâché angels take flight from pine roping atop a gilded 19th-century mirror. A large poinsettia and whimsical papier-mâché reindeer dressed with a red bow decorate a cozy conversation area near the fireplace, and a painted tea table showcases a collection of bottle brush trees and members of the owners' many Christmas "orchestras"—frosted-glass angels made in Europe.

A turn-of-the-century painted leather screen from Italy forms the backdrop for the Christmas
vignette above. The imaginative grouping includes brass candlesticks, bottle brush trees,
and frosted-glass angels playing musical instruments.

Few toys found under the tree on Christmas morning make a child happier than a train set. The tin locomotive above was produced by the Günthermann Company of Nuremberg, Germany, in the early 1900s.

The spirit of a Victorian Christmas pervades this Philadelphia house designed in the Queen Anne style. Built in the 1890s, the stately residence was renovated and decorated to period by its current owners, who stripped down the woodwork and carefully chose the Victorian wallpapers, fixtures, and furniture. "When it came time to celebrate our first Christmas in the house, it was only natural to decorate for the holiday in Victorian style as well," they explain.

The focus of the family's Christmas decor is a balsam fir, which they place in the entrance hall so that it can be seen from all the first-floor rooms. The fragrant tree is trimmed with a mix of ornaments, including family heirlooms, as well as period reproductions and homemade pieces; in Victorian fashion, the tree is set on a table.

Other traditional Victorian Christmas decorations—kissing balls and a winter tree—are found in the living room. Kissing balls, also

Continued

The stained-glass window above, original to the 1890s house, forms a colorful backdrop for an arrangement of toys: a 1940s train set, a tin fire engine, and a 19th-century cast-iron dog.

Many decorations in this Victorian house are sentimental favorites. The village nestled beneath the tree opposite was made by one of the homeowners when he was a child, while the tinfoil star at the top of the tree is a memento from the couple's first Christmas together.

known as kissing boughs or bunches, were usually made by wrapping wooden hoops with mistletoe, holly, or other greens (this family make theirs from boxwood), and sometimes adding ribbons and paper rosettes. According to English custom, the balls were hung, perhaps over a doorway or loveseat, as an invitation to kiss.

The winter tree, above, recalls the Victorian tradition of preserving a Christmas tree from

Continued

Painted white, the elegant "winter tree" above, made from a tree top, is decorated with homemade clay ornaments that were shaped with cookie cutters.

Festoons of boxwood follow the soft draping of the curtains in the living room at left. Dried statice and heather adorn a small tabletop tree.

The dried and bleached ferns above have the fragile appearance of snowflakes. Pinecones, porcelain dolls, and a candle complete the imaginative vignette.

year to year. After the holiday celebrations were over, it was the practice of some people—particularly German settlers in Pennsylvania—to strip the tree of its needles and store the skeleton; the following Christmas, the boughs would be wrapped in cotton batting to simulate snow and the tree redecorated. By the early 1900s, when the natural supply of evergreens was dwindling, it was not unusual for barren trees to be cut down, brought inside, and decorated with batting in the same manner. In lieu of cotton batting, the winter tree made by this family was simply sprayed with white paint. The same frosty look characterizes the dried and bleached ferns that decorate the windowsill above. A larger windowsill display appears in the bedroom at right. Here, a collection of dolls belonging to one of the homeowners, including many favorites that have been passed down through generations, is grouped with poinsettias and greens.

A kissing ball, evergreen boughs, and red and white poinsettias bring a festive look to the Victorian-style bedroom at right.

THOMAS NAST'S CHRISTMAS

"A Visit from St. Nicholas," 1863-1864

Without Thomas Nast, our vision of Santa Claus might be very different. A political cartoonist who originated the familiar symbols of the Republican elephant and the Democratic donkey, Nast is thought to have been the first artist to draw Santa Claus as the "jolly old elf" we know today.

Nast was born in Germany in 1840 and emigrated to New York with his family at age six. As a teenager he enrolled in art school and, at fifteen, began his career as an illustrator. After jobs with several periodicals, he joined *Harper's Weekly* in 1862 as a war correspondent and began to produce acclaimed cartoons and Civil War sketches.

About the same time, Nast "met" Santa when a publisher asked him to illustrate a book of holiday poems that included Clement Moore's "A Visit from St. Nicholas." Combining imagery from Moore's verse, and his childhood memories of Christmas, Nast created a rotund, bearded, pipe-smoking figure in a wooly suit and cap, carrying a large sack of toys (see top row, left).

Nast's first Santa for *Harper's* appeared on January 3, 1863. Santa was shown visiting a Union camp and wearing a suit of stars and stripes (the artist was a staunch Union sympathizer). His next Santa for the magazine, published December 26, 1863, was part of a composite picture that included a soldier home on furlough.

Nast's Christmas illustrations for *Harper's* were so popular that each year for the next twenty-three years the artist would take time from cartooning to contribute holiday drawings to the magazine. At right are just some of those drawings, including the last one Nast did for *Harper's* (bottom row, right). It was published December 28, 1886, and fittingly illustrates a line from Moore's poem.

"Merry Christmas," January 4, 1879

"Caught!" December 24, 1881

"Christmas Post," January 4, 1879

"Merry Old Santa Claus," January 1, 1881

"Not a creature was stirring," December 28, 1886

Christmas
in Santa Fe

On Christmas Eve, the city of Santa Fe and the surrounding countryside sparkle with thousands of *farolitos,* like those in the courtyard of this New Mexico residence. Placed along walls and paths, and on the flat adobe roofs, these "little lanterns" (actually candles set in sand inside paper bags), symbolically light the way for Joseph and Mary in their search for shelter, and herald the arrival of the Santo Niño, or Christ child.

This courtyard fronts a large house in a valley just outside Santa Fe. Designed and built twelve years ago by its present owners, the house recalls the prevalent architectural style of the region—low adobes traditionally built of clay or of bricks made with sun-dried clay and straw—which dates back to the 1600s. The residence is a home to the couple and their three young sons; a separate building serves as a pottery studio. Decorated with the handiwork of craftspeople from Santa Fe and Mexico, the rooms are particularly colorful at Christmas.

Like almost everything else in and around Santa Fe, Christmas festivities are a mix of Indian, Hispanic, and Anglo-American customs. Although the family celebrate with some conventional traditions, like decorating a tree and hanging up stockings, their holiday menu is apt to stray from the standard American fare to include regional New Mexican specialties spiced with red and green chilies. Dinner is usually

Continued

Christmas in New Mexico is not Christmas without the lighting of farolitos like those at left.

Favorites among the family's Christmas decorations are the Mexican tin ornaments above. Pieces like these are available in such shapes as birds, animals, and fish, as well as in more traditional Christmas designs like churches and trees. The shiny embossed tin creates a glittering effect when the ornament is hung on the tree.

followed by a trip to a neighboring pueblo at Tesuque or San Ildefonso to view the seasonal rites of the Turtle Dance or the Evergreen Man. "In many ways," one homeowner says, "the Indian dances give true spirit to the holiday."

Another family tradition involves participation in an annual Christmas fair at which area residents and local craftspeople exchange ornaments of their own making. Many decorations on the family's tree, including cloth Navajo dolls, and small, clay Pueblo Indian figures, have come from the event. Most of the cloth and wooden toys displayed under the tree were also locally made. "On Christmas morning, however," one homeowner says, "the children are more apt to find more contemporary toys." *Continued*

Furnishings designed by one of the owners include the child-size and painted cupboards at right.

Regional accents are also evident in the kitchen, which features traditional southwestern *vigas*, or heavy timbers, spanning the width of the ceiling, and a raised-hearth fireplace in which logs are burned vertically. Red-chili wreaths like those shown here are made throughout the year in Santa Fe, but are particularly popular as decorations at Christmas. Other decorations include Mexican tin and pottery candelabra, a group of Santa figures—including a Santa cat—made by a local craftsman, and stockings with the children's names and birth dates that were knit by an old family friend.

Smoothly rounded with plaster, Santa Fe fireplaces are typically built into a corner or extended into a room, as in the kitchen, above. Decorated for Christmas, this fireplace also has an adjoining banco, or bench—the perfect spot for warming oneself on a chilly holiday evening.

Decorated pottery and tiles made by the homeowners are found in the kitchen, left.

MORE FAST AND FESTIVE DECORATING IDEAS

Evergreens and flowers are natural for a country Christmas celebration.
♦ Here's a clever way to embellish holly and evergreens and create unique wrapping paper at the same time. Spread brown craft paper on a work surface. Lay out the holly and evergreen branches. Spray very lightly with gold and/or silver paint. Allow to dry. Use the greens to decorate a plain wreath or centerpiece. Use the brown paper for gift wrap; the "shadows" of the greens leave pretty patterns on the paper.
♦ Cut flowers during the winter months are truly luxurious. Add just a few blossoms to a ready-made evergreen wreath or to decorate a small topiary tree. Choose lilies or roses and slip the ends of the stems in plastic water reservoirs that you can hide in the center of the greens. At the dining table, a champagne flute with a nosegay of flowers next to each place setting will leave the center of the table open for the Christmas feast.
♦ A practical tip for Christmas decorating is to use pushpins and fine green floral wire for hanging garlands and greens from woodwork.

From the soft glow of candles to the bright twinkle of colored lights on the tree, Christmas is the season of light.
♦ Combine candle colors and a collection of candlesticks in a cluster for a side table. Mix cream and white candles with silver and glass sticks, or red, rose, and pink candles with porcelain sticks. Bayberry green and blue candles are beautiful with old wooden sticks made from thread spools and surrounded by bayberry and blue spruce branches.
♦ For added glow over the dining table, place gold-foil-lined lampshades over chandelier lights. A dimmer switch will offer further atmospheric control.
♦ Create the translucent beauty of a stained-glass window with a product called Gallery Glass Window Color and liquid leading available in craft stores. You can do this on an existing window or recycle a discarded window sash. Check catalogs or magazines for designs. Enlarge

the design on a copy machine to fit the window and then apply liquid leading and colors.

Instead of placing Christmas cards in a box or basket, use them to add color and cheer to a room with one of these clever display techniques.

◆ Punch holes in the upper left corner of each card. Tie them with ribbon onto a garland of greenery on the staircase, mantel, or around a doorway.

◆ Hang a table runner on a wall or door. With gold straight pins, pin all your Christmas cards to the runner for a dramatic display.

◆ Save your favorite Christmas cards and cut them into pleasing shapes or outlines. Border them with old-fashioned tinsel, crepe paper, or ribbon. They make great tree ornaments.

A beautiful setting adds to the enjoyment of Christmas parties and dinners.

◆ During the year search for interesting or antique fabrics to use as runners on the holiday table. One yard of fabric will make a 15-inch-wide hemmed runner 6 feet long. Seam it at the center and make points at each end. Finish the ends with a tassel.

◆ For a festive table, instead of a cloth runner, wire pine wreaths together, making the runner long enough to drape down each side of the table. Cover the wire with red ribbon. Tie a bow at each end. Place a serving bowl or pedestal plate in the center of each wreath.

Displaying collectibles is one of the delights of the season.

◆ Cover coffee cans, canisters, and small gift boxes with Christmas wrap or fabric.

◆ Instead of grouping a collection of Santas or antique toys on a mantel or tabletop, place one on each step of a staircase. If the length of each step goes beyond the balusters, place the object on this outer edge. This will make them more visible and less likely to be stepped on accidentally.

◆ Display a collection of antique bottles or recycle new screw-top bottles by filling with water and a few drops of red, green, or yellow food coloring. Tie Christmas ribbon or raffia around the neck and place them on a windowsill. They look wonderful when the sunlight shines through them.

◆ Create a cheery display of crocheted or knitted afghans in a red wagon and place near the fireplace so you can easily reach for one when you want to snuggle by the fire.

Setting the Christmas Table

Clever Trimmings and New Traditions for Holiday Meals

A beautiful Christmas table adds to the pleasure of the meal and the celebration of the occasion. While tradition is important, witty twists and fresh ideas will delight family and friends and prevent the annual event from becoming ho-hum.

This chapter looks at holiday tables, both casual and formal, in seven homes: The settings display distinctive approaches to entertaining for dinner, brunch, and even a children's holiday tea. Whether your country home is farmhouse rustic or Victorian cozy, you'll discover many clever ideas for decorating the table, from mixing and matching similar china patterns and using fruits and greenery as centerpieces to displaying collectibles and creating mini-vignettes. So that your own Christmas table can be as memorable, we show you how to make a sparkling holiday centerpiece. Indeed, here you will find all the ingredients you need for an outstanding country Christmas setting.

Fruit-shaped ornaments and variegated ivy make an unusual Christmas centerpiece.

Family Traditions

Spode Christmas dinner-ware, above, is used each holiday season. The 19th-century silver napkin rings were collected one at a time. "Each is engraved with an old-fashioned name like Neddy or Herman," says one homeowner. "We all like discovering whose name we've got each year."

When Christmas dinner is served in this Wisconsin house, it includes an element of surprise. A cranberry torte—an old family favorite that completes the meal—is baked with a penny in it; whoever finds the penny is assured luck for the coming year.

The family, in fact, celebrate Christmas with many unique decorating traditions. Every year the owners showcase their collection of early glass and fabric Santa ornaments on the six-foot antique feather tree in a corner of the dining room. All the ornaments are small, in keeping with the delicate scale of the tree. A garland of colored glass beads and old-fashioned clip-on candles provide the finishing touches. A painted child's sled, topped with a collection of 19th century toy sheep and a Santa figure crafted by a family friend, makes an unusual centerpiece.

At left, an 18th-century
American swing-leg cherry
dining table is set for Christmas dinner. The Norwegian
table runner, woven in a
reindeer pattern, and the
Irish crystal goblets represent two branches of
the family tree.

A Colonial Celebration

Wine is served, above, from the top of a 1690 Hadley chest. Holly and poinsettias are displayed in an English delft vase and bowl. The gentleman in the portrait is Colonel Samuel Clark, who purchased the house in 1788.

Candlelight sets a warm tone for a holiday buffet in this Connecticut dining room where four generations of a family gather at Christmas. The table features a fruit pyramid, a type of centerpiece that first became popular in America around 1700. Clusters of holly and boxwood fill the gaps between apples and a pomegranate top, which are pushed onto picks on a conical form. Tiny red berries add sparks of color. Rather than repeat the bright-red candles of the chandelier, subtle rosy-brown candles complement the softer hues of the table.

Boxwood, holly, and apples were used to make the traditional fruit pyramid centerpiece at right.

Country-Store Feast

Santas add a playful charm
to the dining area at right.
Each of the figures is handmade and no two are alike.
Dried pomegranates deco-
rate the garland draped
from the counter.

This Chester County, Pennsylvania, dining area is the center of a great deal of entertaining at holiday time. On Christmas Eve the homeowners, their children, and their grandchildren get together here for a light dinner that is likely to feature shrimp and other hors d'oeuvres, soup, and a dessert such as chocolate fondue. A cranberry punch, which both the children and the adults can enjoy, is served from an antique yellowware bowl.

Around the room are a variety of Christmas decorations, including a group of wood, fabric, and cornhusk Santas, all made by contemporary craftspeople whose work the couple sell at their country store.

Housed in the same large stone 1759 building as the residence, the store provides an excuse for a second holiday party. At this occasion, friends and customers are invited to a "Candlelight Christmas" open house. The entire shop and house are lit solely by candles placed in the windows, on tabletops, and in chandeliers. Between 200 and 300 people come by to enjoy wassail and hot mulled cider, and to have a peek at the family Christmas tree decorated with old-fashioned handmade ornaments. "I knew the party was going well," one homeowner says, "when a girl came up to me and said, 'this place is like fairyland, it's exactly what Christmas should look like.'"

Above, an antique yellowware bowl serves as a holiday centerpiece when surrounded by princess pine, fruit, nuts, rose hips, and cinnamon sticks. The contemporary sgraffito plates are made by a Texas potter.

Cildren love to have their own grown-up parties: this Pennsylvania dining room is the setting for a child-size Christmas tea. Although the tree is decorated for the entire family's enjoyment, its painted fraktur ornaments and gingham hearts are particularly appealing to children.

On the table, the menagerie centerpiece was assembled from a collection of contemporary folk art. An antique Gaudy Welsh tea service will be used to serve cocoa, and spatterware plates are soon to be filled with sandwiches, Christmas cookies, and a taste of fruitcake made from a hundred-year-old family recipe.

On the side table at left sits a contemporary bird tree, a traditional form of Pennsylvania folk art.

Part of the centerpiece for a children's Christmas tea party, the little wooden house above is actually an antique sewing box; the hinged roof opens. The plates, cups, and saucers are contemporary spatterware.

Christmas Romance

Three different patterns of antique French porcelain are combined in the holiday place settings above. As a romantic touch, pink carnations and white pine are tied with ribbon to lace-edged linen napkins.

The owners of this Massachusetts house do quite a bit of entertaining throughout the year, but Christmas dinner, they say, is reserved just for the immediate family.

For this occasion, they set an elegant Christmas table in the living room. A collector of American furniture and "almost everything that's pretty," one of the homeowners loves to decorate the table—a New York Federal-period piece—with some of her favorite treasures. A romantic holiday look is created by mixing tableware patterns that share the themes of lace, flowers, and pastel colors. The unusual pink-gold candlesticks and cornucopia vases are Steuben art glass from the 1920s decorated with contrasting colored-glass vines and flowers, and filled with holiday sprays of white pine, cedar, and deep-pink roses. At each place setting, American swirled cranberry-glass goblets are paired with engraved crystal stemware.

The traditional Christmas dinner regularly includes an old family recipe for fresh cranberry frappé—a sherbetlike ice served in little glass cups—which accompanies the main dish of roast turkey or sliced tenderloin of beef. And among the special desserts that are offered each year is the family favorite—homemade pecan pie, with a dollop of whipped cream.

116

Complementing the elegant table setting, the porcelain angels on the mantel at left are part of a collection of angel orchestras set out each Christmas.

SUGAR-GLAZED FRUIT

Sugar-glazed fruit shown off in a silver basket or in a porcelain bowl is one of the prettiest holiday table decorations you can make. It is also among the easiest: all you need are fruits, egg white, and granulated sugar.

Select fruits that vary in color and size, such as red, yellow, and green pears, peaches with a rosy blush, and several types of grapes. You may also want to include some exotic varieties, such as the angular starfruit in the arrangement at left. The fruits should be unbruised and firm, and not fully ripened, or they will turn soft in a day or two.

Make sure the fruits are dry and at room temperature. Pour granulated sugar onto a plate. Mix egg white lightly in a bowl, but do not let it become frothy. (You can judge by eye the quantity of egg white and sugar needed for the amount of fruit being used.) With a pastry brush, coat a piece of fruit with the egg white, roll it in the sugar, and place it on a cake rack to dry. Repeat the process until all the fruits are glazed. Let the fruits sit at room temperature for at least an hour before handling. (Keep in mind that because the egg white is raw and unrefrigerated, glazed fruit should never be eaten; it is a decoration only.) If you place the bowl of sugar-glazed fruit where it catches the light of candles or a chandelier, the sugar will sparkle.

Christmas Eve is the time traditionally reserved by the owners of this Victorian house for their holiday dinner. "On Christmas day," they explain, "it's too hard to get the children back to earth to do anything serious once they open their gifts."

The family's traditional dinner of soup, roast duck or guinea hens, and plum pudding with hard sauce is served in their dining room, which has been restored to period style with eleven different wallpaper patterns on the ceiling and walls. Many of the furnishings are heirlooms, but the couple have also found Victorian pieces, such as the sideboard, at auctions and shows.

At Christmas time, even the decorations in the room have a romantic, old-fashioned look. Garlands around the window and doorway are made with princess pine. Tiny white porcelain birds and red bows are tucked into the greens on the window ledge, and decorative hand-painted compotes are used for the arrangements of fruits and roses on the table and sideboard.

The mirrored sideboard above provides a glimpse of the Christmas tree in the hall. Amaryllis blossoms are arranged in a glass vase, and lusterware is displayed on the shelf over the mirror.

Victorian
Touches

*For Christmas dinner, an
antique crocheted tablecloth
from China is used over a
red liner on the dining room
table at left. The family like
to make frequent use of their
antique tableware, including this gold-and-red
Limoges service.*

New Mexico Flavor

The rabbit plate above is from a special line of Christmas pottery made by the homeowners. Clustered in the centerpiece are a doll-size tea set and bowls, and a miniature black-and-white Acoma Indian pottery jar.

Tucked into a nook under the stairs, the table in this New Mexico kitchen is laid out for a casual Christmas brunch; the blue-painted *banco*, built along the walls, provides plenty of seating. Strings of red, chili-shaped Christmas lights and a cluster of Mexican clay villagers in the window enliven the room.

The table is set with rabbit-motif plates that were made and decorated by the homeowners (who work together as potters) and with chunky blue-and-gold blown-glass goblets. Fruit, pine boughs, and ceramic Nativity figures from Oaxaca make up the centerpiece. The exotic pineapple and bright yellow lemons provide splashes of color amidst the somber greens of the centerpiece. The dramatic lighting is provided by a spotlight mounted behind the overhead beam. Since the fruit and greens are casually arranged, all the perishables can spend the night in the refrigerator and be returned to the table for festive occasions throughout the holiday.

A sunny corner of the kitchen is a comfortable spot for a casual holiday brunch. Much of the artwork that appears in the room, such as the folk-art snake and Rio Grande painting, was made by family members.

Holiday Entertaining

*A Time for Warm Welcomes
and Merry Feasting*

Amid all the hustle and bustle of holiday preparations, renewing old friendships and family relationships provides one of the season's deepest delights. Conviviality and good cheer permeate the air and give rise to rounds of festive parties, get-togethers, and reunions. The days leading to Christmas and New Year's are ripe with opportunities to offer warm welcomes, share fond memories, and engage in merry feasting in the spirit of the season.

Ring in the Yuletide by having loved ones, young and old, help to trim the tree, then reward them with a generous buffet supper and brandied eggnog. Or, give yourself and guests a break from the busy pace with the relaxation and friendly conversation of a simple fireside supper.

As befits the highlight of the season, Christmas dinner is a splendid affair with roast goose and wild rice-chestnut stuffing. Celebrate New Year's Eve with traditional glitter and gaiety. And to mark the end of the holiday festivities, observe Twelfth Night, on the fifth of January, with a special dinner.

A plump roast goose with all the trimmings is the highlight of a Christmas buffet dinner.

TREE TRIMMING PARTY

Chicken-Vegetable Soup

Spinach and Bacon Salad with Garlic Croutons

Spicy Beef Pasties

Brandied Eggnog

Party Gingerbread Cookies

SERVES 6

▼

Kick off the Christmas season with a tree trimming party: Invite friends to help you hang your own ornaments or ask them to bring along homemade decorations such as popcorn balls or cranberry garlands. Your guests might also enjoy spending part of the evening creating their own ornaments or treats to take home: Set out tubes of colored icing, dried fruit, and candies to decorate gingerbread cookies, or provide materials and instruction books for making festive origami figures.

Whatever the plan, this type of casual buffet is an easy way to entertain during the hectic holiday period. Have bowls of oranges, apples, popcorn, and candy canes—seasonal symbols in themselves—available for nibbling throughout the evening. Serve the soup in mugs, and the pasties—beef-filled turnovers—on a platter, to be eaten with either forks or fingers. Everything can be prepared ahead of time, and each of the recipes in this menu can easily be doubled for a larger group.

Chicken-Vegetable Soup

Cauliflower, carrots, and kale are widely available in winter, but ripe tomatoes may be hard to find. Canned tomatoes (preferably Italian-style plum tomatoes) may be used instead. This chunky soup can be prepared, through Step 3, a few days ahead of time; add the chicken, parsley, and seasonings just before serving.

3 tablespoons vegetable oil
2 medium leeks, coarsely chopped (about 2 cups)
3 cloves garlic, minced
8 cups canned chicken broth
2 cups drained, coarsely chopped canned tomatoes, or 3 medium fresh tomatoes, seeded and chopped
2 cups cauliflower florets

2 medium carrots, diced (about 1¼ cups)
4 large kale leaves, shredded, or 3½ cups shredded cabbage
1 teaspoon marjoram or oregano
½ cup elbow macaroni or other small pasta
2 cups diced cooked chicken (about 10 ounces)
¼ cup chopped parsley
½ teaspoon pepper
Salt

1. In a stockpot or large saucepan, heat the oil over medium heat. Add the leeks and garlic, and sauté until translucent, about 5 minutes.

2. Add the chicken broth, tomatoes, cauliflower, carrots, kale, and marjoram, and bring to a boil. Reduce the heat to medium-low, cover, and simmer the soup for 10 minutes.

3. Increase the heat to medium-high. When the soup comes to a full boil, stir in the macaroni, and cook, uncovered, for 8 minutes.

4. Stir in the chicken, parsley, pepper, and salt to taste. When the soup returns to a boil, reduce the heat to medium and simmer the soup until the chicken is heated through, about 2 minutes longer.   *6 servings*

Chicken-Vegetable Soup

Spinach and Bacon Salad with Garlic Croutons

Spinach—especially the curly-leaved type—must be washed carefully, or you risk getting bits of grit in your salad. The easiest method is to plunge the trimmed leaves into a sinkful of lukewarm water to which a little salt has been added. Swish the spinach around in the water, then leave it for a moment to let the sand settle to the bottom. Lift out the leaves, drain and rinse the sink, and repeat this process until no grit remains. To lighten your last-minute workload, wash the spinach a day in advance; shake it dry, roll it in paper towels, then place it in a plastic bag and refrigerate until needed.

GARLIC CROUTONS
Six ½-inch-thick slices firm whole-wheat bread
½ cup olive oil
¼ cup chopped parsley
2 cloves garlic, minced
½ teaspoon pepper

SALAD AND DRESSING
¼ pound bacon
½ pound fresh spinach

1 large tomato, cut into wedges
1 red onion, thinly sliced
⅔ cup olive oil
⅓ cup lemon juice
4 teaspoons Dijon mustard
½ teaspoon salt
½ teaspoon pepper
3 hard-cooked eggs, coarsely
    chopped

1. Preheat the oven to 375°. Line a baking sheet with foil.
2. Make the croutons: Cut the bread into cubes. In a medium bowl, stir together the olive oil, parsley, garlic, and pepper. Add the bread cubes and toss until well coated.
3. Spread the bread cubes in an even layer on the prepared baking sheet and bake for 15 to 20 minutes, or until golden.
4. Meanwhile, make the salad: In a medium skillet, cook the bacon over medium heat until crisp, about 10 minutes. Drain the bacon on paper towels; crumble and set aside.
5. Tear the spinach into bite-size pieces and place them in a large salad bowl.
6. Add the tomato and onion slices to the spinach; set aside.
7. Make the dressing: In a small bowl, whisk together the olive oil, lemon juice, mustard, salt, and pepper.
8. Just before serving, add the chopped eggs, crumbled bacon, and croutons to the salad. Pour the dressing over the salad and toss well. Serve immediately.

6 servings

In The Country Kitchen, Della Lutes recalled her mother's full-bodied vegetable soup, which you "had to chew a little. . . . This soup was the dinner. No Melba toast accompanied it, nor any . . . other supplementary starches . . . . It was served in a huge china tureen and ladled into soup plates of generous size. It was 'eaten' with a spoon, but whether from the side, tip, or whole spoon I do not remember. I only remember that it was . . . licking good!"

Spicy Beef Pasties

Pasties, popularized in this country by 19th-century immigrants from Cornwall, England, were the lunchtime fare of Cornish miners. Unlike the traditional meat pies, which are quite mild in flavor, these are spiced with lively Mexican seasonings—chilies, coriander, cumin, and oregano.

PASTRY
2 cups flour
⅔ cup yellow cornmeal
¼ cup chopped fresh coriander
1½ teaspoons salt
6 tablespoons chilled butter, cut into pieces
6 tablespoons chilled vegetable shortening
8 to 10 tablespoons ice water

FILLING AND GLAZE
1 small potato
½ pound ground beef
1 medium carrot, diced
1 cup chopped scallions
3 cloves garlic, minced
1 can (4 ounces) diced mild green chilies, drained
¼ cup chopped fresh coriander
1½ teaspoons ground cumin
1 teaspoon oregano, crumbled
½ teaspoon salt
½ teaspoon pepper
1 egg, lightly beaten

1. Make the pastry: In a large bowl, stir together the flour, cornmeal, coriander, and salt. With a pastry blender or two knives, cut in the butter and shortening until the mixture resembles coarse crumbs.

2. Sprinkle 8 tablespoons of the ice water over the mixture and toss it with a fork. The dough should be moistened just enough so that it holds together when it is formed into a ball. If necessary, add up to 2 tablespoons more water. Form the dough into a flat disk, wrap in plastic wrap, and refrigerate for at least 30 minutes, or until well chilled.

3. Meanwhile, make the filling: Peel and quarter the potato, then thinly slice each quarter. In a large bowl, combine the potato, ground beef, carrot, scallions, garlic, and green chilies. Add the coriander, cumin, oregano, salt, and pepper, and mix gently until well combined.

4. Preheat the oven to 375°. Line a baking sheet with foil and lightly grease the foil.

5. On a lightly floured surface, roll out the dough to a ¼-inch thickness. Using a saucer or a paper template, cut out twelve 5-inch rounds. Reroll and cut any scraps.

6. Spoon about ¼ cup of filling onto one side of each pastry round, leaving a ½-inch border around the edge. Brush the edge of the pastry with water, then fold the pastry to cover the filling, forming semicircular turnovers. Seal the edges by pressing them with the tines of a fork.

7. Place the pasties on the prepared baking sheet. Prick the tops of the pasties with a fork, then brush them with the beaten egg. Bake for 30 to 35 minutes, or until the pasties are golden brown. Serve hot, or at room temperature.   *Makes 12 pasties*

Spicy Beef Pasties and Spinach and Bacon Salad with Garlic Croutons

Brandied Eggnog and Party Gingerbread Cookies

Brandied Eggnog

This traditional recipe can be made richer by replacing some of the half-and-half with heavy cream. For an even thicker eggnog, whip the cream lightly before adding it.

2 cups milk	*¾ cup sugar*
1 cinnamon stick	*2 cups half-and-half or light cream*
1 vanilla bean, split (optional)	*¾ cup rum*
3 whole cloves	*¾ cup brandy*
Pinch of mace	*1½ teaspoons vanilla extract*
6 egg yolks	*About 1 teaspoon nutmeg*

1. In a heavy saucepan, combine the milk, cinnamon stick, vanilla bean (if using), cloves, and mace. Place the pan over very low heat and cook for 5 minutes.

2. Meanwhile, in a medium bowl, whisk together the egg yolks and sugar until well blended.

3. Increase the heat under the saucepan to medium and bring the milk to a simmer. Very gradually add the hot milk to the egg-yolk mixture, whisking constantly, then return the mixture to the saucepan and cook, stirring constantly, until the mixture is thick enough to coat the back of a wooden spoon, 2 to 3 minutes. Do not let the mixture boil.

4. Strain the eggnog into a large bowl and set aside to cool to room temperature.

5. Stir in the half-and-half, rum, brandy, vanilla extract, and ½ teaspoon of the nutmeg. Cover the bowl and refrigerate the eggnog for at least 2 hours, or overnight. Just before serving, dust the top with additional nutmeg to taste. *6 servings*

Party Gingerbread Cookies

Decorate these cookies lavishly with icing and bits of dried fruit, or colored sugar and candies. You can use a heavy-duty plastic food storage bag as a disposable decorating bag: fill it with icing, then snip a tiny hole in one corner and squeeze the icing out through the opening. Note that a fairly wide range is given for the amount of flour in this recipe: the humidity, as well as the type of flour, can cause variations in the consistency of the dough. For cookies that are crisp but not hard, add just enough flour to make the dough manageable; chilling it as directed will help, too. And try to use as little flour as possible when rolling and cutting the dough.

2⅓ to 3 cups flour

2 teaspoons ginger

1 teaspoon cinnamon

½ teaspoon salt

1 stick (4 ounces) butter, softened to
    room temperature

¾ cup (packed) dark brown sugar

¼ cup molasses

1 egg

DECORATION AND ICING

Dried fruit, cut into small pieces

Slivered almonds

Shredded coconut

1¼ cups confectioners' sugar

2 tablespoons water

¼ teaspoon vanilla extract

1. In a medium bowl, stir together 2⅓ cups of the flour, the ginger, cinnamon, and salt; set aside.

2. In a large bowl, cream the butter and brown sugar. Stir in the molasses, then add the egg. Gradually add the flour mixture, beating well after each addition. Beat in up to ⅔ cup more flour, if necessary, until the dough is no longer sticky.

3. Turn the dough out onto a lightly floured surface and knead it lightly until smooth, about 2 minutes. Form the dough into a ball, flatten it into a disk, wrap it in plastic wrap, and refrigerate it for at least 1 hour, or overnight.

4. Preheat the oven to 350°. Lightly grease a baking sheet.

5. On a lightly floured surface, using a lightly floured rolling pin, roll out the dough to a ¼-inch thickness and cut it with floured cookie cutters. Place the cookies on the prepared baking sheet, leaving 1 inch of space between them, and decorate with dried fruit, almonds, and coconut. Gather, reroll, and cut the scraps of dough.

6. If you plan to string the cookies on ribbons for hanging, use a skewer or ice pick to pierce small holes at the tops of the cookies. Bake the cookies for 15 to 17 minutes, or until crisp.

7. Let the cookies cool on the baking sheet for 2 to 3 minutes, then transfer them to a rack to cool completely. If the holes have closed up, repierce them while the cookies are still warm.

8. Meanwhile, prepare the icing: In a small bowl, combine the confectioners' sugar, water, and vanilla, and stir until thick and smooth; set aside.

9. Fill a decorating bag or tube with the icing and pipe it onto the cookies. Add details with more bits of the dried fruit, if desired.   *Makes 2 to 3 dozen cookies*

The 1912 book **Fairs and Fetes**, *which suggested themes for charity bazaars, proposed a preholiday Fair of the Christmas Shops. One booth would be The Bake-Shop, displaying "all sorts of Christmas cakes . . . with an edge of holly made of candied cherries . . . fancy cookies of all kinds, and especially gingerbread men made to represent Santa Claus, decorated in icing—tracery of features, buttons and bag of presents on his back."*

SKATING PARTY
SUPPER

Lamb Stew with Winter Vegetables

Rice-Corn Bread

Thyme Butter

Mixed Green Salad

Apple Crumb Pie with Walnut Crust

SERVES 6

▼

A moonlight skating party would be a fanciful and romantic prelude to this meal, but an afternoon of any winter sport—cross-country skiing, hiking, or simply playing in the snow—calls for just such a hearty supper. Set the kitchen table with whimsical winter accessories, such as sparkling snow domes and snowflake candleholders, then gather your friends for a warming repast. The main dish is lamb stew, made with parsnips and winter squash and served with fresh, hot bread and herbed butter. A salad of watercress or other tart greens would help offset the richness of the stew.

Later, after games or conversation—or another quick trip outdoors to admire a starry winter sky—finish the meal with steaming mugs of coffee (spiked with applejack, if you like) and generous slices of apple pie.

Lamb Stew with Winter Vegetables

Although most vegetables, from asparagus to pumpkins, are available fresh, frozen, or canned all year round, it's very much in the country spirit to honor the traditional seasons of the garden. Acorn squash and parsnips, called for in this recipe, are typical "winter vegetables." In days gone by, they would have been stored in the root cellar, to furnish the table through the months when the garden was buried under snow. You can make this winter-worthy lamb stew in advance and reheat it at serving time; in fact, its flavor will improve if you do so. Don't be put off by the quantity of garlic called for; slow cooking mellows its flavor to a savory sweetness.

Your attic (or your child's toy chest) might yield charming accessories like the baby- and doll-sized caps, socks, and gloves that warm this winter table. If no such diminutive creations turn up, make a survey of local thrift shops—or knit your own.

¾ cup flour

1 teaspoon salt

½ teaspoon pepper

3 pounds stew lamb, cut into 2-inch chunks

4 tablespoons oil

6 medium parsnips, peeled and cut into
    1½-inch chunks (about 2 cups)

1¼ cups chopped leeks

15 cloves garlic, peeled

1 can (35 ounces) whole tomatoes, with
    their juice

2 teaspoons thyme

1 medium acorn squash, quartered,
    peeled and cut into ½-inch-thick slices

½ pound small mushrooms

2 tablespoons chopped parsley, for garnish

1. In a shallow bowl, combine the flour, salt, and pepper. Dredge the lamb in the seasoned flour, tapping off the excess; reserve the excess flour.

2. In a Dutch oven or flameproof casserole, heat 3 tablespoons of the oil over medium-high heat. Add the lamb to the pan and cook until the meat is evenly browned, about 8 minutes.

3. Stir in the reserved seasoned flour mixture, and cook, stirring, until the flour is absorbed. Add the parsnips, leeks, garlic, and remaining 1 tablespoon oil, reduce the heat to medium, and cook, stirring, for 10 minutes.

4. Stir in the tomatoes with their juice and the thyme, and bring the liquid to a boil over medium-high heat. Cover the pan, reduce the heat to medium-low, and simmer until the vegetables are slightly softened, about 20 minutes.

5. Add the acorn squash and mushrooms, and cover the pan. Cook, stirring occasionally, until the lamb is tender, another 40 minutes.

6. Ladle the stew into shallow soup bowls and serve hot, garnished with the parsley.

6 servings

Rice-Corn Bread

This bread is based on an old South Carolina recipe called "philpy," which was made with white rice and rice flour. Here, brown rice is combined with cornmeal for a more healthful bread with a slightly nutlike flavor.

2 cups white cornmeal
1½ teaspoons baking powder
1½ teaspoons baking soda
1 teaspoon salt

2 cups cooked brown rice
1½ cups buttermilk
2 eggs, lightly beaten
2 tablespoons butter, melted

1. Preheat the oven to 450°. Butter two 8 x 2-inch round cake pans.
2. In a medium bowl, blend the cornmeal, baking powder, baking soda, and salt; set aside.
3. In a large bowl, mash the rice with a wooden spoon. (Or, pulse it in a food processor for about 15 seconds.) Add the buttermilk, eggs, and butter.
4. Add the dry ingredients to the rice mixture and beat until well blended. Pour the batter into the prepared pans and spread it evenly with a rubber spatula. Rap the pans once or twice on the counter to remove any air pockets.
5. Bake for 30 minutes, or until the breads pull away from the sides of the pans and the tops are light golden. Serve hot.   *Makes two 8-inch round loaves*

A dinner party is the perfect time to show off a collection of favorite objects, like the snow domes above. Or, revive the old dinner-party custom of giving favors: Set a small, inexpensive gift at each guest's place.

Thyme Butter

Easy to make, savory herbed butter is a wonderful complement to fresh, hot bread. You can substitute another herb, such as oregano, basil, or tarragon, if you prefer. Should there be any leftover thyme butter, it can be spread on toast or used to dress cooked green vegetables or potatoes.

1 stick (4 ounces) unsalted butter,
*   softened to room temperature*

2 tablespoons chopped fresh thyme, or
*   1 teaspoon dried*

1. In a small bowl, stir together the butter and thyme until well blended.
2. Cover the bowl and refrigerate for at least 3 hours, or up to 1 week (the flavor will intensify with time). The butter may also be frozen for up to 2 months.
3. Let the butter return to room temperature before serving.   *Makes ½ cup*

Apple Crumb Pie with Walnut Crust

Although apples are available all year round, they are at their best soon after the harvest in the autumn and early winter. What better time to make this delicious dessert? Flavored with walnuts, this pie's crumbly topping is like the crust of an apple crisp. Serve the pie slightly warm, topped with whipped cream or vanilla ice cream.

PASTRY
⅔ cup finely chopped walnuts
1 cup flour
½ teaspoon salt
2 tablespoons dark brown sugar
3 tablespoons chilled butter, cut into pieces
2 tablespoons chilled vegetable shortening
3 to 4 tablespoons ice water

FILLING
3 tablespoons flour
3 tablespoons dark brown sugar
1 teaspoon cinnamon

1 cup light or dark raisins (optional)
3 large Granny Smith or other flavorful
   apples (about 1½ pounds)

TOPPING
½ cup flour
⅓ cup (packed) dark brown sugar
⅓ cup chilled butter
½ cup coarsely chopped walnuts
½ teaspoon cinnamon
½ cup heavy cream
1 tablespoon confectioners' sugar

1. Preheat the oven to 375°.

2. Make the pastry: Spread the walnuts in a shallow baking pan and toast them in the oven, stirring occasionally, for 10 to 12 minutes, or until golden brown; set aside to cool slightly. Turn off the oven.

3. In a large bowl, combine the cooled walnuts, the flour, salt, and brown sugar. With a pastry blender or two knives, cut in the butter and shortening until the mixture resembles coarse crumbs.

4. Sprinkle 2 tablespoons of the ice water over the mixture and toss it with a fork. The dough should be just barely moistened, enough so it will hold together when it is formed into a ball. If necessary, add up to 2 tablespoons more water, 1 tablespoon at a time. Form the dough into a flat disk, wrap in plastic wrap, and refrigerate for at least 30 minutes.

5. Meanwhile, make the filling: In a large bowl, stir together the flour, brown sugar, cinnamon, and raisins, if using; set aside.

6. Peel, core, and thinly slice the apples, then add them to the flour mixture and toss until well coated; set aside.

7. Preheat the oven to 375°.

8. On a lightly floured surface, roll the dough out to a 12-inch circle. Fit the dough into a 9-inch glass pie plate. Trim the overhang to an even ½ inch all the way around. Fold the overhang under and crimp the dough to form a decorative border. Prick the pastry with a fork.

9. Spoon the apple mixture into the pie shell, mounding it toward the center. Pat the filling down gently without compacting it.

10. Make the topping: In a small bowl, combine the flour and brown sugar. Using a pastry blender or two knives, cut in the butter until the mixture resembles coarse crumbs. Stir in the walnuts and cinnamon.

11. Sprinkle the topping over the filling, covering it completely, and bake for 45 to 55 minutes, or until the apples are tender and the topping begins to brown.

12. Just before serving, in a medium bowl, whip the cream with the confectioners' sugar until stiff. To serve, cut the pie into wedges and top each serving with a dollop of whipped cream.

Makes one 9-inch pie

Apple Crumb Pie with Walnut Crust

FIRESIDE SUPPER

Cider-Glazed Fresh Ham

Sautéed Apple Slices

Turnip Purée with Scallion Crisps

Broccoli with Lemon • Tossed Green Salad

Pear-Hazelnut Upside-Down Cake

SERVES 6

▼

For the hostess whose home has a fireplace, the Christmas season presents many opportunities to share the comforts of the hearth. Take the time to prepare the fire carefully, so that a strong, clear blaze will burn throughout the evening with minimal attention. Welcome your guests into a house filled with the tantalizing aromas of roast ham and winter fruits and vegetables, then sit down at a table set in front of the fire. Or, serve the supper on trays or tray tables arranged close to the hearth.

A golden pear upside-down cake brings a meal to a delicious close. Spice the after-dinner coffee or tea with cardamom, cinnamon sticks, or cloves, and follow it with a fireside session of charades—or simply good, relaxed conversation. If you don't have a fireplace, enjoy this supper where you can watch the sunset, or just sit in the coziest corner of your living room, by lamplight or candle glow.

Cider-Glazed Fresh Ham

Fresh ham is the term used for uncured leg of pork. It is cooked the same way as beef or veal, not like cured ham. For this recipe, choose a bone-in ham weighing 6 to 8 pounds. Don't worry if you can only find a larger ham; the leftovers are delicious.

6- to 8-pound fresh ham
1 teaspoon salt
½ teaspoon pepper
24 whole cloves

2 cups apple cider
1 cup dark beer
3 tablespoons brown sugar

1. Preheat the oven to 450°.

2. Trim the outer skin and fat from the ham, leaving ¼ inch of fat around the bone area. Rub the ham with the salt and pepper, and stud it with the cloves.

3. Place the ham on a rack in a roasting pan, put it in the oven, and immediately reduce the oven temperature to 325°. Bake the ham for 15 minutes.

4. Meanwhile, in a small bowl, stir together the cider, ¾ cup of the beer, and the sugar. After the ham has baked for 15 minutes, pour the cider glaze over it. Bake the ham, basting it with the pan juices every half hour, for 4 to 4½ hours, or until a meat thermometer inserted into the ham (not near the bone) registers 170°.

5. Transfer the ham to a platter and let it stand for 15 minutes before carving.

6. Meanwhile, make the gravy: Skim off as much fat as possible from the juices in the roasting pan. Add the remaining ¼ cup beer and place the pan over medium heat, stirring to scrape up the brown bits that cling to the pan. Cook over low heat until hot, about 1 minute.

7. Carve the ham and serve it with the gravy.

6 servings

Sautéed Apple Slices

Pork and ham are often paired with fruit accompaniments. Here, unpeeled apple slices are sautéed in butter and flavored with nutmeg and brandy. This tasty side dish will bring a touch of color to the meal.

1 Red Delicious apple
1 Golden Delicious apple
2 tablespoons butter

1 tablespoon brown sugar
¼ teaspoon nutmeg
2 tablespoons apple brandy

1. Core and thinly slice the unpeeled apples. In a large nonstick skillet, melt the butter over medium heat. Add the apple slices and cook, stirring, until the apples begin to brown, 2 to 3 minutes.

2. Add the brown sugar, nutmeg, and brandy, and cover the pan. Reduce the heat to low and cook until the apples are just tender, 1 to 2 minutes. Stir the mixture, then serve the apples with pan juices spooned over them.

6 servings

Robust red wines go well with fall foods. For a festive look, wrap the bottle in a large cloth napkin. First, fold the napkin in half diagonally, then "diaper" the bottle with it. Bring the points around to the front and tie them in a square knot.

Turnip Purée with Scallion Crisps

Since the oven will be needed for baking the ham until just 15 minutes before serving time, prepare this recipe through Step 3 before putting the ham in the oven. Make the scallion topping (and reheat the turnip purée, if necessary), while the ham rests prior to carving. The batter-fried scallion crisps make a tasty addition to other mashed or creamed vegetables; try them with sweet or white potatoes, carrots, or winter squash.

3 pounds white turnips
1 tablespoon water
⅓ cup butter
3 tablespoons heavy cream
1½ teaspoons salt
½ teaspoon white pepper

⅓ cup yellow cornmeal
⅓ cup flour
1 bunch scallions, cut into 2-inch pieces
   (about 1 cup)
2 eggs, lightly beaten

1. Preheat the oven to 350°.
2. Peel the turnips and cut them into ¼-inch-thick slices. Place the slices in a single layer in a baking pan, sprinkle them with the water, and cover with foil. Bake for 25 to 30 minutes, or until tender when pierced with the tip of a sharp knife.
3. Place the turnips in an ovenproof bowl and mash them with a potato masher until smooth, then stir in 3 tablespoons of the butter, the cream, 1 teaspoon of the salt, and the pepper. Cover the bowl to keep the purée warm.
4. Just before serving, reheat the turnip purée, if necessary.
5. Meanwhile, in a small bowl, stir together the cornmeal, flour, and the remaining ½ teaspoon salt.
6. In a medium skillet, heat the remaining butter over medium heat. Dip the scallions into the beaten eggs, shake them to remove the excess, then roll them in the cornmeal mixture. Fry the scallions in the butter, turning them frequently, until crisp and golden, about 5 minutes.
7. Chop the fried scallions and sprinkle them over the turnip purée.

6 servings

The patterns on your linens, china, and flatware may suggest decorative touches that will help coordinate the tablesetting. Here, the gold cord design of the plate is echoed by lengths of gold drapery cord tied around each napkin.

Pear-Hazelnut Upside-Down Cake

TOPPING

1 large, firm Bartlett pear

2 tablespoons flour

4 tablespoons butter, softened to room
  temperature

⅓ cup sugar

½ cup chopped hazelnuts

CAKE

2¼ cups flour

1¼ teaspoons baking powder

¾ teaspoon baking soda

1½ teaspoons cinnamon

¾ teaspoon ginger

½ teaspoon salt

6 tablespoons butter, softened to room
  temperature

½ cup sugar

3 eggs

½ teaspoon almond extract

¾ cup buttermilk, or ¾ cup milk plus 2¼
  teaspoons vinegar

1 cup chopped hazelnuts

1. Preheat the oven to 350°.

2. Make the topping: Core the unpeeled pear and cut it into ¼-inch-thick slices. Dredge the pear slices in the flour; set aside.

3. In a 9-inch ovenproof skillet with straight sides, melt the butter over medium heat. Add the sugar, and cook, stirring constantly, until the sugar dissolves and the mixture is golden brown, about 4 minutes.

4. Remove the skillet from the heat. Arrange the pear slices, overlapping slightly, in a circular pattern over the sugar mixture and press them down gently. Sprinkle the pears with the hazelnuts; set aside.

5. Make the cake: In a medium bowl, stir together the flour, baking powder, baking soda, cinnamon, ginger, and salt; set aside.

6. In a large bowl, cream the butter until fluffy. Gradually beat in the sugar, then add the eggs, one at a time, and continue beating until the mixture is light and fluffy. Beat in the almond extract.

7. Alternating between the two, add the dry ingredients and the buttermilk, beating well after each addition. Stir in the hazelnuts.

8. Spread the batter evenly over the pear layer. Rap the skillet gently once or twice on the counter to remove any air pockets. Bake for 40 to 45 minutes, or until the cake shrinks from the sides of the skillet and a toothpick inserted in the center of the cake comes out clean and dry.

9. Immediately run the tip of a knife around the edge of the skillet to loosen the cake, then carefully turn it out onto a plate. Serve the cake warm, or at room temperature.

Makes one 9-inch cake

FIREPLACE TREATS

For a welcome change from fancy holiday affairs, entertain friends with a hearthside party featuring desserts cooked over the fire. A snapping blaze in a country fireplace is a magnet for guests, evoking thoughts of treats such as popcorn and toasted marshmallows. (Note: Sample these desserts only if you burn wood in your fireplace; do not cook over the flames of an artificial log.)

S'mores need no introduction for anyone who has ever been to Scout camp, but the basic recipe—a toasted marshmallow and a piece of chocolate sandwiched between graham crackers—is open to creative interpretation. Try chocolate-coated graham crackers, or add peanut, almond, or cashew butter, or sliced bananas, to the "filling."

Toasted marshmallows become Shaggy Dogs when dipped in melted chocolate and then in shredded coconut. And if you've mastered the art of toasting bread over a fire, sample this slightly more sophisticated creation: Spread a slice of lightly toasted bread with butter and marmalade, then enfold a golden-brown melted marshmallow in the toast.

Popcorn is one of the simplest of fireplace foods: A long-handled popping basket shaken over the fire pops crisp popcorn. Flavor with cinnamon-sugar butter, honey, molasses, or melted chocolate or simply toss with chocolate chips or chopped peanuts.

Fresh fruits are delicious when toasted over a fire. Chunks of pineapple, apple, and pear, or whole strawberries, cherries, and fresh figs can be threaded on metal skewers and basted with a mixture of honey and melted butter. Or, sprinkle the fruit with brown sugar, which will caramelize over the fire. Dried fruits can be presoaked or simmered in wine or fruit juice, then cooked on skewers.

When you have a good hot fire going, you can also bake fruit on the hearth. Fill cored apples with raisins, brown sugar and rum, wrap them in heavy-duty foil, and place them at the base of the fire to bake. Peeled bananas, brushed with lemon juice, rum, and melted butter, and sprinkled with brown sugar and spices, can be wrapped and cooked the same way.

If only "chestnuts roasting on the open fire" will do, just slash their shells with a sharp knife, place them in a long handled corn popper (or wrap in a sheet of heavy foil with holes punched in it), and roast them 4 inches from the fire for 15 to 20 minutes.

To accompany your hearthside desserts, serve fine-quality coffee or tea spiced with cardamom, cinnamon, or cloves.

A CHRISTMAS BUFFET

Oysters on the Half Shell

Roast Goose with Wild Rice-Chestnut Stuffing

Melange of Vegetables with Tarragon Butter

Angel Biscuits

Cranberry-Apple Tart with Walnut Crust

Vanilla Ice Cream • Spiced Coffee

Champagne

SERVES 8

▼

After the merry hubbub of Christmas morning—fancy ribbons and pretty papers flying, exclamations of delight and thanks—anticipation turns to the splendors of the Christmas dinner. While buffets are usually associated with casual entertaining, with a carefully selected menu and charming table-top accessories, a buffet can be as grand as any sit-down dinner. Perfect for homes without formal dining rooms, the flexibility of buffet service is also ideal for young families where the children are usually more interested in the distractions of the morning's gifts than in enjoying a formal dinner.

This Christmas menu features a fragrant Roast Goose with Wild Rice-Chestnut Stuffing, along with sautéed vegetables, and a festive fruit tart that is delicious served with vanilla ice cream. Oysters on the half shell make an elegant starter for the meal and cranberry relish and biscuits complement the main dishes.

While this meal is easy to prepare—the goose is only slightly more complicated to roast than a turkey—it does require time and planning. The stuffing takes about 1 hour to make. The goose roasts for a little over 4 hours and sits for another 30 minutes before carving. Although the biscuits take only a few minutes to bake, they need time to rise.

Oysters are their best during the winter months, but like all seafood are at their peak flavor when eaten soon after purchasing. Buy them at the last minute, no more than 2 days before serving.

Don't forget to leave time to set an attractive table. Here, in keeping with the less formal style of a buffet, cleverly mixed and matched serving dishes and linens beautifully contrast, yet complement, the simple wood table. Fresh flowers and soft candlelight are always lovely, while the crystal compote filled with colorful Christmas ornaments adds a touch of holiday fun.

Roast Goose with Wild Rice-Chestnut Stuffing

"There never was such a goose! Bob said he didn't believe there ever was such a goose cooked. Its tenderness and flavour, size and cheapness, were the themes of universal admiration."
—*A Christmas Carol* by Charles Dickens

To make your buffet table especially festive, tie glittery ribbons around napkins and silverware. For convenience, place the napkins and silver in a basket, or in individual tall glasses.

1 goose, about 14 pounds, giblets and neck trimmed and reserved
1 teaspoon salt
1 teaspoon pepper
Wild Rice-Chestnut Stuffing (see next page)
1 ½ cups canned chicken broth
1 small onion
12 juniper berries, crushed
1 bay leaf
1 cup water
3 tablespoons flour

1. Preheat oven to 400°. Cut off and discard excess fat from cavity of goose. Rinse and dry goose and sprinkle cavity with salt and pepper. Loosely stuff goose with about 10 cups Wild Rice-Chestnut Stuffing, then truss opening with skewers and string. Place remaining stuffing in greased baking dish and cover with foil; set aside.

2. Prick skin of goose all over with fork to allow excess fat to drip off during cooking. Place goose, breast-side up, on rack in deep roasting pan, and roast for 20 minutes.

3. Reduce oven temperature to 325°, cover goose loosely with foil, and roast for an additional 17 minutes per pound (about 4 hours and 20 minutes total for a 14-pound goose). Remove foil after 2 hours. Using basting bulb or cooking spoon, periodically remove fat from roasting pan, leaving cooking juices in pan. Carefully pour hot fat (there may be as much as 1 quart) into large can or foil pan to cool and solidify before discarding it. Goose is done when skin is browned, drumstick moves easily in its socket, and juices run clear when goose is pierced with a sharp knife; internal temperature should register 180°.

4. While goose cooks, in small saucepan bring giblets and neck, chicken broth, whole onion, juniper berries, bay leaf, and water to a boil over medium-high heat. Cover pan tightly, reduce heat to low, and simmer gently for about 1 hour. Strain broth, reserving giblets and neck; discard other solids. Remove meat from neck and chop neck meat and giblets. Set aside broth and chopped neck meat and giblets.

5. One hour before goose is done, place reserved dish of stuffing in oven.

6. When goose is cooked, transfer to carving board and cover loosely with foil; let rest for 30 minutes before carving.

7. To make gravy, reheat giblet broth over low heat. Pour off all but ¼ cup of liquid from roasting pan. Place roasting pan over medium heat and slowly stir in flour. Cook, stirring frequently, until flour is lightly browned, about 1 minute.

8. Add reheated broth and reserved chopped neck meat and giblets, stirring constantly. Simmer gravy until it has thickened and lost any taste of uncooked flour, 5 to 7 minutes. Stir to blend thoroughly; season with additional salt and pepper, if desired. Keep gravy warm over very low heat while you carve the goose.

Wild Rice-Chestnut Stuffing

Wild rice is a classic accompaniment to game birds and poultry. This dish adds savory sausage and sweet chestnuts with tantalizingly delicious results.

4 cups canned chicken broth

1 cup raw wild rice, rinsed

1 cup raw brown rice

2 tablespoons butter

2 tablespoons olive oil

3 medium-size leeks (white part only), washed and coarsely chopped (about 1 pound), or 4 cups chopped onions

1 pound country-style sausage, casings removed

$^1/_2$ pound fresh mushrooms, coarsely chopped

1 can (10 ounces) chestnuts packed in water, drained, or 35 whole chestnuts, cooked, shelled, and halved

2 cups diced carrots

$^1/_2$ cup chopped parsley

2 teaspoons crumbled sage

$^1/_2$ teaspoon pepper

1. In medium-size saucepan, bring broth to a boil over medium heat. Stir in wild rice and brown rice, cover pan, reduce heat to medium-low, and simmer until rices are tender and most of liquid is absorbed, 35 to 40 minutes. Remove pan from heat; set aside.

2. In large skillet, melt butter in oil over medium-high heat. Add leeks and sauté until they are well coated with butter, 1 to 2 minutes.

3. Add sausage, breaking it up with a spoon. Add mushrooms and cook until sausage is no longer pink, 5 to 10 minutes. Remove skillet from heat.

4. Stir in cooked rice, chestnuts, carrots, parsley, sage, and pepper. Let stuffing cool slightly before using.   *Makes about 16 cups*

Melange of Vegetables with Tarragon Butter

The mild anise-like flavor of tarragon perfectly complements this combination of red onions, broccoli, and bell peppers. Walnuts provide nice crunchy texture to the dish.

2 tablespoons butter

2 tablespoons olive oil

1 red onion, thinly sliced

2 cloves garlic, crushed through a press

4 cups broccoli florets

2 large red bell peppers, slivered (about 2 cups)

2 large yellow or green bell peppers, slivered (about 2 cups)

1 tablespoon chopped fresh tarragon, or $^1/_2$ teaspoon dried

$^1/_2$ teaspoon salt

$^1/_4$ teaspoon pepper

1 cup walnut halves

1. In large skillet, melt butter in oil over medium-high heat. Add onion and garlic, and cook, stirring, until onion begins to wilt, 1 to 2 minutes.

2. Add broccoli and bell peppers, and cook, stirring, until vegetables are just tender, 5 to 7 minutes.

3. Stir in tarragon, salt, and pepper, then sprinkle walnuts over vegetables. Serve immediately.   *8 servings*

Angel Biscuits

This recipe is also called Bride's Biscuits because the use of yeast, in addition to baking soda, guarantees light biscuits, even for novice cooks.

2 tablespoons lukewarm (105° to 115°) water
1 package active dry yeast
1 tablespoon sugar
2¹/₂ cups flour
¹/₂ teaspoon baking soda

¹/₂ teaspoon salt
¹/₃ cup chilled butter, cut into tablespoons
1 cup buttermilk, or 1 cup milk plus 1 table
    spoon vinegar

S *piced coffee is a pleasing end to a holiday dinner. To prepare it, in a mug stir together 1 tablespoon each maple syrup and heavy cream. Add a pinch each of ground cloves and ginger, and fill the mug with hot coffee. Stir again and let stand 1 to 2 minutes. Garnish the mug with an orange slice or cinnamon stick, and top the coffee with a dollop of whipped cream, if desired.*

1. Place the water in a small bowl and sprinkle the yeast over it. Add a pinch of the sugar and let stand until the yeast begins to foam, about 5 minutes.

2. In a medium bowl, stir together the flour, the remaining sugar, the baking soda, and salt. Using a pastry blender or two knives, cut in the butter until the mixture resembles coarse meal.

3. Add the buttermilk and then the yeast mixture and stir just until a soft dough forms. Transfer the dough to a lightly floured surface and knead until smooth, about 2 minutes. Form the dough into a ball and place it in a large, greased bowl. Cover the bowl with a slightly dampened kitchen towel, set it aside in a warm, draft-free place, and let the dough rise until it doubles in bulk, 45 minutes to 1 hour.

4. Punch the dough down, then transfer it to a lightly floured surface. Using a lightly floured rolling pin, roll out the dough to a ¹/₂-inch thickness. With a 2-inch round biscuit cutter, cut out 24 biscuits. Gather, reroll, and cut any scraps.

5. Place the biscuits on an ungreased baking sheet and set aside, uncovered, in a warm, draft-free place to rise until almost doubled in bulk, about 30 minutes.

6. Preheat the oven to 400°. Bake the biscuits for 10 to 12 minutes, or until golden brown.

Makes 24 biscuits

Cranberry-Apple Tart with Walnut Crust

Tart Granny Smith apples and cranberries are combined for his grand finale to the Christmas menu. Not-too-sweet, it provides a palate-pleasing contrast to the richness of the roast goose and wild rice-chestnut stuffing.

PASTRY

²/₃ cup chopped walnuts
1 cup flour
2 tablespoons sugar
¹/₄ teaspoon salt
¹/₃ cup chilled butter, cut into pieces
2 to 3 tablespoons ice water

FILLING

3 Granny Smith apples (about 1 pound),
  peeled and sliced ¹/₄ inch thick
2 tablespoons flour
¹/₃ cup plus 2 tablespoons sugar
2 teaspoons grated orange zest
1 cup fresh or frozen cranberries
¹/₄ cup orange juice
1 teaspoon cornstarch

1. Make the pastry: In food processor, process walnuts, pulsing machine on and off until walnuts are coarsely ground. Add flour, sugar, and salt, and pulse just until mixed, 2 to 3 seconds. Add butter and pulse until mixture resembles coarse cornmeal, 5 to 10 seconds. With processor running, add just enough ice water to form a cohesive dough. Remove dough from processor, form into a ball, flatten into a disk, and wrap in plastic wrap. Refrigerate for at least 30 minutes, or until well chilled.

2. Meanwhile, in large bowl, toss apples with 2 tablespoons of the sugar and 1 teaspoon of the orange zest; set aside

3. Preheat oven to 375°.

4. Roll dough into an 11-inch circle and fit it into a 9-inch tart pan with removable bottom. Trim overhang. Fill pastry with apple mixture. Bake for 25 minutes.

5. Meanwhile, in small saucepan, combine cranberries, remaining ¹/₃ cup sugar, 1 teaspoon orange zest, orange juice, and cornstarch, and stir to dissolve cornstarch and sugar. Cook over medium heat, stirring constantly, until mixture comes to a boil and thickens, about 5 minutes. Remove pan from heat.

6. When tart has baked for 25 minutes, spoon cranberry mixture evenly over apples and bake for another 10 minutes, or until crust is golden and apples are tender.

7. Transfer tart to rack to cook for 15 minutes before removing sides of pan. Leave tart on pan bottom to serve. *Makes one 9-inch tart*

NEW YEAR'S EVE DINNER

Nantucket Scallop Soup

Herbed Cornish Hens with

Brown Rice and Chestnut Stuffing

Green Beans in Shallot Butter

Lettuce and Cherry Tomato Salad · Dinner Rolls

Caramel Custards with Warm Apricot Compote

SERVES 4

▼

New Year's Eve is the quintessential occasion for an elegant dinner party. Instead of a big bash, plan an intimate gathering for four. Start off the evening with a glass of champagne and keep the bubbly flowing throughout the meal—it complements every course.

You'll probably want to serve this dinner late, so that you finish at midnight in time for a New Year's toast. The late dinner hour will allow you plenty of time during the day for leisurely preparation of the food and the special setting. What makes this holiday table unique is its golden glow: Choose flatware and china with brass, bronze, or gold accents, and use metallic-threaded linens. Complement these accessories with a centerpiece of gilded nuts, pine cones, and fruit; tie golden ribbons on the stems of the glasses; and spill handfuls of gold and silver stars across the table.

155

Nantucket Scallop Soup

This light yet creamy soup is made with bay scallops; if only the larger sea scallops are available at your market, cut them into quarters before cooking them.

2 cups bottled clam juice
2 cups milk, scalded
2 cups peeled, diced red potatoes
1 cup chopped onion
2 cloves garlic, minced
1 bay leaf

½ pound bay scallops
⅓ cup chopped carrot
½ teaspoon salt
¼ teaspoon white pepper
⅓ cup finely chopped scallions

    1. In a medium saucepan, combine the clam juice, milk, potatoes, onion, garlic, and bay leaf, and bring to a simmer. Cover the pan and cook until the potatoes are tender, about 30 minutes.

    2. Pour the soup through a sieve set over a bowl. Remove and discard the bay leaf. Using a wooden spoon, press the cooked vegetables through the sieve. Return the soup to the pan.

    3. Bring the soup to a boil, then reduce the heat so the soup simmers. Add the scallops, carrot, salt, and pepper, and cook for 5 minutes longer. Ladle the soup into individual soup plates, sprinkle each serving with the chopped scallions, and serve.

4 servings

When serving champagne, remember that slender "tulips" or "flutes" conserve the wine's evanescent bubbles better than saucer-shaped glasses. Choose the thinnest crystal possible and be sure it is immaculate.

Herbed Cornish Hens with Brown Rice and Chestnut Stuffing

Choose smooth, glossy chestnuts that feel heavy in your hand. They can be prepared ahead of time, but be sure to peel them while they are still warm. The shells are quite difficult to remove once the chestnuts have cooled.

STUFFING
1 pound unshelled chestnuts (about 36)
½ pound country-style bulk sausage
1 cup coarsely chopped onion
3 cups cooked brown rice (1 cup raw)
1 cup coarsely chopped celery
2 tablespoons chopped parsley
1 teaspoon sage, crumbled
1 teaspoon salt
¾ teaspoon pepper
½ teaspoon thyme

CORNISH HENS AND GRAVY
2 large Cornish hens, rinsed
1 teaspoon salt
¼ cup chopped parsley
3 cloves garlic, minced
1 teaspoon sage, crumbled
½ teaspoon pepper
1 medium onion, thinly sliced
½ cup canned chicken broth
1 tablespoon cornstarch

1. Make the stuffing: Using a sharp paring knife, cut an X in the flat side of each chestnut shell. Place the chestnuts in a medium saucepan and add cold water to cover. Bring the water to a boil and cook for 20 to 25 minutes. Drain the chestnuts in a colander and cool them briefly under cold running water. While the chestnuts are still warm, remove the shells and peel off the paperlike skin.

2. Set the chestnuts aside to cool slightly, then coarsely chop them.

3. If the sausage is in a casing, remove and discard the casing. Crumble the sausage into a large, heavy skillet. Add the onion and cook over medium-high heat for 5 minutes, stirring occasionally.

4. Add the chopped chestnuts, brown rice, celery, parsley, sage, salt, pepper, and thyme, and toss lightly with two forks until very well combined. There should be about 5 cups of stuffing.

5. Preheat the oven to 425°.

6. Prepare the Cornish hens: Sprinkle the cavity of each hen with ½ teaspoon of salt. Fill each hen with about 1 cup of stuffing. Place the remaining stuffing in a greased baking dish, cover with foil, and set aside.

7. Truss the hens and rub them with the parsley, garlic, sage, and pepper. Place the onion slices in the bottom of a large roasting pan. Place the hens on top of the onions.

8. Roast the hens for 20 minutes, then reduce the oven temperature to 350°. Place the dish of stuffing in the oven. Roast the hens and stuffing for 40 to 45 minutes. Baste the hens occasionally with the pan juices while cooking. The hens are done when an instant-reading meat thermometer inserted into the thickest part of the thigh registers 165° and the juices run clear when the same area is pierced with the tip of a knife.

9. Transfer the hens to a warm serving platter and cover with foil to keep warm.

10. For the gravy, transfer the pan juices and onions to a small saucepan. In a small bowl, stir together the broth and cornstarch, then add this mixture to the pan. Bring to a simmer over medium-high heat and cook, stirring, until thickened, 2 to 3 minutes.

11. To serve, remove the trussing strings from the hens. Cut the hens in half and pour the gravy over them. Serve the extra stuffing on the side.   *4 servings*

Some stationery stores offer pretty, ready-made place cards. If you prefer to make your own, keep a supply of patterned papers, cards, and metallic or fabric trimmings on hand and you'll be able to create personal place cards for any occasion.

Green Beans in Shallot Butter

Sautéed shallots dress up these crisp-tender green beans. If you can find small, slender beans, cook them whole; halve or sliver the beans if they are large or thick. For a dash of extra color, add some yellow wax beans to this side dish.

1 pound green beans
2 tablespoons butter
2 tablespoons olive oil

½ cup chopped shallots (about 3 ounces)
½ teaspoon salt
½ teaspoon pepper

1. Cut the green beans into 2-inch lengths.
2. In a medium skillet, heat the butter and oil over medium heat. Add the shallots and sauté until light golden, about 5 minutes.
3. Add the green beans, salt, and pepper, and sauté until the beans are crisp-tender, 3 to 5 minutes longer. Serve hot.

4 servings

This 1911 exaltation of a midnight supper could well have been written about a New Year's Eve party: "The most enjoyable of all meals is that which is served as the clock strikes twelve. There is a delightfully effervescent gaiety in the air, and a flavor to the food which is lacking at other times. Even bread and butter or crackers and cheese taste like ambrosia, while daintier food has a flavor surpassing that mythical delicacy."

Caramel Custards with Warm Apricot Compote

As in the classic recipe for *crème caramel,* a layer of sugar in the bottom of each dish turns into a luscious caramel sauce for these custards. When the desserts are unmolded, the sauce coats the custard. If you prefer to serve the custards without unmolding them, the caramel will be a sweet surprise at the bottom of each dish.

CARAMEL CUSTARDS
¼ cup (packed) light brown sugar
4 eggs
3 tablespoons maple syrup
1½ cups heavy cream
½ teaspoon vanilla extract

APRICOT COMPOTE
¼ pound dried apricots
1 cup cranberry juice
½ teaspoon grated lemon zest
½ cup fresh or frozen cranberries (optional)
1 tablespoon dark rum

1. Make the custards: Place 1 tablespoon of the brown sugar in the bottom of each of 4 individual soufflé dishes or 6-ounce custard cups. Spread the sugar into a smooth, even layer; set aside.
2. Preheat the oven to 350°.
3. In a large bowl, beat the eggs until light. Stir in the maple syrup, cream, and vanilla, and continue beating until well blended. Divide the custard evenly among the prepared dishes. Set the dishes in a roasting pan placed on the middle rack of the oven. Pour hot water into the pan to reach halfway up the sides of the dishes.
4. Bake the custards for 35 to 40 minutes, or until they are firm and the tip of a knife inserted into the center comes out clean.
5. While the custards are baking, make the apricot compote: In a medium saucepan, combine the apricots, cranberry juice, and lemon zest. Bring to a boil, then

reduce the heat, cover the pan, and simmer until the apricots are very tender, about 20 minutes. If using cranberries, add them to the apricot mixture 5 minutes before it is done. Set the mixture aside, uncovered, to cool slightly.

6. Using a potato masher, mash the apricots in the cooking liquid, leaving the fruit somewhat chunky. Stir in the rum, cover the pan, and set aside.

7. When the custards are done, remove them from the hot water bath and wipe the soufflé dishes dry. Immediately unmold the custards by running the tip of a knife around the edge of each dish, then carefully inverting the dish onto a dessert plate. Spoon some apricot compote over each custard and serve warm.   *4 servings*

Caramel Custards with Warm Apricot Compote

TWELFTH NIGHT DINNER

Mulled Wine · Smoked Fish Canapés

Roast Pork Loin with Sage

Prunes and Apricots in Port Wine

Sautéed Bell Peppers with Tarragon

Potato Cakes with Scallion Sour Cream

Chocolate-Almond Torte

SERVES 6

▼

Twelfth Night, celebrated on January fifth (the eve of Epiphany), is a time for festive dinners and parties. In some countries, gifts are exchanged on this occasion rather than on Christmas, and the traditional King's Cake is shared: the finder of the lucky bean baked into the cake is crowned King (or Queen). However you mark it, Twelfth Night provides a happy note on which to bring the holiday season to a close.

A suitable starter for this winter night's gathering is mulled red wine, accompanied with an appetizer of your choice. Smoked salmon with herbed cream cheese and cocktail breads is one luxurious and delectable possibility. Set a regal table, with touches of scarlet and gold and, if possible, a kingly crown. Conclude the meal with a luscious version of King's Cake: a dense chocolate-almond torte, topped with a glossy chocolate glaze.

Mulled Wine

Combining the wine with the fruit and spices a day in advance ensures that it will become thoroughly infused with their flavors. To retain as much as possible of the wine's alcohol content, keep the pot covered from start to finish. If you uncover it, especially while heating the wine, the alcohol will quickly begin to evaporate.

4 small apples
24 whole cloves
Two bottles (750 ml each) burgundy or
*   other full-bodied red wine*
4 medium oranges, sliced

2 cups orange juice
4-inch piece fresh ginger, thinly sliced
4 small cinnamon sticks
⅔ cup sugar

1. Stud each apple with 6 cloves. Place the apples in a large nonreactive pot and add one bottle of the wine, the orange slices, orange juice, ginger, and cinnamon sticks. Cover the pot and let stand at room temperature for at least 12 hours.

2. At serving time, add the second bottle of wine and the sugar, and stir well. Bring the mixture to a boil over high heat, then immediately remove the pot from the heat. Strain the mulled wine into a heatproof pitcher or punch bowl, and serve.

Makes about 12 cups

This advice, from the 1909 Handbook of Hospitality for Town and Country, is, if anything, truer than ever today. "Our hostess will be wise if she does not attempt to do too many things on the day when she expects guests to dinner. . . . In order to make a dinner a delightful occasion, the lady of the house must be at her best, fresh and in good spirits. . . . It is better to have fewer persons present or fewer courses than to lose one's astral calm."

Roast Pork Loin with Sage

Buy a rolled and tied boneless pork loin for this recipe; it's easy to carve and there is no waste. Be careful not to overcook the pork, as this cut is quite lean; the meat should reach an internal temperature of no higher than 170°.

2 tablespoons olive oil
6 cloves garlic, minced
¼ cup chopped fresh coriander
1 tablespoon sage, crumbled

1 teaspoon salt
1 teaspoon pepper
4-pound center-cut boneless
*   pork loin*

1. Preheat the oven to 450°.

2. In a small bowl, combine 1 tablespoon of the oil, the garlic, coriander, sage, salt, and pepper, and mash the mixture to a paste.

3. Rub the remaining 1 tablespoon oil all over the pork loin, then rub the garlic mixture over the surface of the meat. Place the pork loin in a shallow roasting pan and pour in ½ cup of water. Place the pork loin in the oven and roast it for 20 to 25 minutes, basting several times.

4. Reduce the oven temperature to 325° and roast the pork for 1 hour to 1 hour and 10 minutes, or until an instant-reading meat thermometer registers 165° to 170°.

5. Let the pork stand at room temperature for 5 minutes before carving.

6 servings

The Twelfth Night dinner

Prunes and Apricots in Port Wine

This dried-fruit compote not only provides the perfect accompaniment to roast pork, but it can also be served as a dessert at another meal. You might like to offer the remaining port as an after-dinner drink. Its sweet, mellow flavor is certain to be welcomed on a chilly winter's night.

1 pound dried apricots
1 pound pitted prunes

2 cups port wine
2 tablespoons grated lemon zest

1. In a medium nonreactive saucepan, combine the apricots, prunes, port, and lemon zest, and bring to a boil over medium heat.

2. Reduce the heat to low, cover the pan, and simmer until the fruit is tender, about 15 minutes. If not serving immediately, transfer the fruit and liquid to a bowl, cover, and refrigerate.

Makes about 6 cups

Sautéed Bell Peppers with Tarragon

Red and yellow bell peppers are now available all year round in many supermarkets. Some stores offer orange, purple, and chocolate-brown peppers, as well.

3 tablespoons olive oil
2 red onions, thinly sliced
6 cloves garlic, minced
2 large green bell peppers, thinly sliced
2 large red bell peppers, thinly sliced

2 large yellow bell peppers, thinly sliced
2 teaspoons tarragon
¾ teaspoon salt
½ teaspoon black pepper
½ cup canned chicken broth

1. In a large skillet, heat the oil over medium heat. Add the onions and garlic, and sauté until light golden, about 5 minutes.

2. Add the bell peppers, tarragon, salt, and black pepper, and sauté until the peppers are coated with oil, 2 to 3 minutes longer.

3. Add the chicken broth, cover the pan, and cook until the peppers are limp, 1 to 2 minutes longer.

6 servings

Potato Cakes with Scallion Sour Cream

These lacy potato pancakes are topped with a savory sour cream. Do not grate the potatoes too far in advance, as they will begin to darken if left standing too long.

SCALLION SOUR CREAM
½ cup sour cream
½ cup finely chopped scallions
¼ teaspoon pepper

POTATO CAKES
2 pounds all-purpose potatoes

2 eggs, lightly beaten
¼ cup flour
2 cloves garlic, minced
½ teaspoon salt
½ teaspoon pepper
2 to 3 tablespoons olive oil

1. Make the scallion sour cream: In a small bowl, combine the sour cream, scallions, and pepper, and stir until blended. Cover and refrigerate until needed.

2. Peel the potatoes, then grate them on the coarse side of a grater into a large bowl. Add the eggs, flour, garlic, salt, and pepper, and stir until well blended.

3. Heat 1 teaspoon of the oil in a large, heavy nonstick skillet over medium heat. Drop ¼-cup portions of the potato mixture into the skillet and flatten each portion into a cake. Cook the potato cakes until the edges are crisp and browned, 3 to 4 minutes, then turn them and cook until golden brown, 3 to 4 minutes longer. Transfer the cooked potato cakes to a warm platter and cover them with foil to keep warm. Cook the remaining potato mixture in the same fashion, adding more oil as necessary to prevent sticking.

4. Serve the potato cakes with the scallion sour cream.

6 servings

A "jeweled" crown can be purchased at a costume or novelty shop, or, with a little ingenuity, made at home from foil, a scrap of velvet, and some old costume jewelry. The embroidered "royal" emblems—which can be attached to ribbons to serve as napkin rings—come from a notions counter.

Chocolate-Almond Torte

This nontraditional King's Cake (it's usually a ring of brioche) plays a pivotal role in the holiday celebration: A dried bean is baked into it, and when the cake is cut, the person who receives the slice containing the bean rules the day. Just a word of caution: Be sure to warn your guests about the bean before they take a bite of cake!

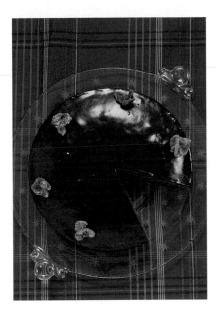

1 cup blanched whole almonds (about 4½ ounces)
1½ cups confectioners' sugar
3 whole eggs plus 1 egg white
⅔ cup flour
⅓ cup unsweetened cocoa powder
½ teaspoon baking powder
1½ sticks (6 ounces) butter, softened to room temperature
½ teaspoon almond extract
1 dried white bean, such as Great Northern
2 ounces semisweet chocolate, cut into pieces
¼ cup heavy cream
Candied violets, for garnish (optional)

1. Preheat the oven to 350°. Butter an 8 x 2-inch round cake pan, line the bottom with buttered waxed paper, and then flour the pan.

2. Place the almonds in a food processor and process, pulsing the machine on and off, for 5 to 10 seconds, or just until the almonds are finely ground. Do not overprocess or the nuts will turn into an oily paste.

3. Add the sugar and egg white, and pulse just until combined; set aside.

4. In a small bowl, stir together the flour, cocoa, and baking powder.

5. In a large bowl, combine the almond mixture with the butter and beat until creamy and light. Add the whole eggs, one at a time, beating well after each addition, then beat in the almond extract.

6. Gradually add the dry ingredients, beating just until combined; do not overbeat. Drop the bean into the batter and stir gently.

7. Spread the batter evenly in the prepared pan. Rap the pan once or twice on the counter to remove any air pockets. Bake for 30 to 35 minutes, or until the cake shrinks from the sides of the pan and a toothpick inserted in the center of the cake comes out clean and dry.

8. Let the cake cool in the pan on a rack for 15 minutes, then turn it out onto the rack to cool completely.

9. When the cake is cool, make the chocolate glaze: Place the chocolate and cream in a double boiler and heat over simmering water, stirring often, until the chocolate has melted and the mixture is smooth.

10. Remove the waxed paper from the cake, leaving the cake on the rack. Place a large sheet of waxed paper under the rack.

11. Pour the glaze onto the center of the cake and tilt the rack to allow the glaze to coat the entire top and sides (to keep the glaze smooth, do not attempt to spread it). Leave the cake on the rack until the glaze has set, or refrigerate it for a few minutes to set the glaze more quickly. When the glaze is firmly set, transfer the cake to a serving plate. Decorate the cake with candied violets, if desired. *Makes one 8-inch cake*

This single-layer almond-chocolate torte, enrobed in a chocolate glaze, is adorned with crystallized violets. If you prefer to decorate the cake with a lacy white pattern instead, place a doily on top and dust sifted confectioners' sugar over it, then carefully remove the doily.

Holiday Baking

Sweet Treats and Indulgences
from Country Kitchens

Sugarplums may no longer be the treats that children dream of, but sweet indulgences have always been one of the pleasures of the holiday season. As frigid winter winds whip across the fields and streets, what could be more cozy than a country kitchen infused with the sweetly spicy aroma of freshly baked cookies? Here we bring you many Christmas favorites from gingerbread cookies to dream bars. The holiday season is the perfect opportunity for a cookie-baking fest. Invite friends to bring their favorite recipes and spend a fun-filled afternoon baking and decorating batch after batch of cookies. Of course, taste-testing the delectable results is a must, so have a pot of fresh-brewed coffee or mulled cider ready.

This chapter also offers a selection of spectacular desserts to present as the grand finale to holiday fare—from a classic Southern bourbon-pecan pie to a luscious orange-chocolate cake. Quick breads are always perfect as thoughtful gifts for the busy hostess. And to make your baked goods look as good as they taste, you'll find some bright ideas for wrappings and containers.

Crisp gingerbread cookies are classic Christmas treats.

Gingersnaps

For a crunchy topping, sprinkle these cookie-jar favorites with sugar while they are still warm. For a decorative design, use a drinking glass with a pressed or cut pattern, or a cookie stamp, to flatten the balls of dough.

2 cups flour
2 teaspoons ground ginger
1 teaspoon baking soda
¼ teaspoon salt
⅓ cup butter, softened to room
*   temperature*

⅓ cup vegetable shortening
1 cup (packed) dark brown sugar
1 egg
¼ cup molasses
2 tablespoons granulated sugar
*   (optional)*

1. Preheat the oven to 350°. Lightly grease a baking sheet.
2. In a small bowl, stir together the flour, ginger, baking soda, and salt.
3. In a large bowl, cream the butter, shortening, and brown sugar. Add the egg, and beat until light and fluffy, about 3 minutes. Beat in the molasses. Gradually add the dry ingredients, beating well until the dough is smooth.
4. Shape the dough into 1-inch balls and place them on the prepared baking sheet, leaving 2 inches of space between them. Flatten them to a ¼-inch thickness by pressing them with the bottom of a glass dipped in cold water. Bake for 9 to 11 minutes, or until the cookies are slightly puffed.
5. Transfer the cookies to a rack and, if desired, sprinkle them with the granulated sugar while still warm.

Makes about 4½ dozen

Spritz Cookies

Cookies formed with a cookie press (which extrudes the dough through a patterned disk) are called *spritz*, the German word for "squirt." The buttery dough is usually flavored simply with vanilla, allowing the swirled shapes of the cookies to take center stage. A chocolate glaze and a dusting of chopped almonds add a finishing touch.

COOKIES
2 cups flour
½ teaspoon baking powder
2 sticks (8 ounces) butter, softened to
*   room temperature*
⅓ cup sugar
1 egg
½ teaspoon vanilla extract

GLAZE
3 ounces semisweet chocolate
4 teaspoons vegetable
*   shortening*
⅓ cup finely chopped blanched
*   almonds*

1. Preheat the oven to 350°. Lightly grease a baking sheet.
2. Make the cookies: In a small bowl, stir together the flour and baking powder.

In a large bowl, cream the butter and sugar until light and fluffy. Beat in the egg and vanilla. Gradually beat in the dry ingredients, beating well after each addition until the dough is smooth.

3. Fill a cookie press with the dough and form the cookies on the prepared baking sheet, leaving 1 inch of space between them. Bake for 11 to 13 minutes, or until the edges are just beginning to turn golden.

4. Let the cookies cool on the baking sheet for 2 to 3 minutes, then transfer them to a rack to cool completely before dipping them in the glaze.

5. Meanwhile, make the glaze: In the top of a double boiler over hot, not simmering, water, melt the chocolate and vegetable shortening and stir until smooth. Place the chopped almonds in a small bowl. Dip the cookies halfway into the glaze, then into the chopped almonds. Return the cookies to the rack until the glaze is set.

Makes about 3 dozen

Lemon Sugar Cookies

These are truly old-fashioned cookies: simple, crisp, and not overly sweet. Refrigerate the dough overnight—or for at least a few hours—so that it will be easier to handle and will require minimal flour for the rolling process.

2 cups flour
½ teaspoon baking soda
½ teaspoon cream of tartar
¼ teaspoon salt
1 stick (4 ounces) butter, softened to room temperature

1 teaspoon grated lemon zest
½ teaspoon vanilla extract
1 cup plus 2 tablespoons sugar
1 egg
2 tablespoons milk

1. In a small bowl, stir together the flour, baking soda, cream of tartar, and salt.

2. In a large bowl, cream the butter. Beat in the lemon zest and vanilla, then beat in 1 cup of the sugar. Beat in the egg and milk.

3. Gradually beat in the dry ingredients, beating well after each addition until the dough is smooth.

4. Turn the dough out onto a sheet of plastic wrap and form it into a ball. Wrap the dough and refrigerate it for at least 2 hours, or overnight.

5. Preheat the oven to 375°. Lightly grease a baking sheet.

6. Cut the dough into thirds; wrap two portions in plastic wrap and return them to the refrigerator. On a lightly floured surface, using a floured rolling pin, roll one portion of dough out to a ⅛-inch thickness.

7. Cut out the cookies using a floured 3-inch round cookie cutter. Gather, reroll, and cut any scraps. Transfer the cookies to the prepared baking sheet, leaving 1 inch of space between them. Bake for 10 to 12 minutes, or until the edges are just beginning to brown. Transfer the cookies to a rack and sprinkle them with the remaining 2 tablespoons sugar while still warm. Let the cookies cool completely.

8. Store the cookies in an airtight container.

Makes about 3 dozen

Gingerbread Cookies

Although gingerbread figures are a symbol of Christmas, it's fun to bake these cookies in other shapes for other holidays and special occasions. Indeed today, cookie cutters can be found in many designs, from dinosaurs to dump trucks. If you have antique cookie cutters, don't be afraid to use them for baking. Just be sure to dry them well after washing so that they do not rust. See Royal Icing Decoration (pages 88-89) for some cookie-decorating ideas.

COOKIES

1 stick (4 ounces) butter
⅓ cup molasses
½ cup (packed) light brown sugar
1 tablespoon ground ginger
½ teaspoon cinnamon
½ teaspoon ground cloves
½ teaspoon nutmeg
½ teaspoon baking soda
1 egg, lightly beaten

2½ cups flour
¼ teaspoon baking powder
¼ teaspoon salt

DECORATION AND ICING

Dried fruits, cut into small pieces
1¼ cups confectioners' sugar
2 tablespoons water
¼ teaspoon vanilla extract

1. Preheat the oven to 325°. Lightly grease a baking sheet.

2. Cut the butter into 1-inch pieces and place them in a large bowl.

3. In a medium saucepan, bring the molasses, brown sugar, ginger, cinnamon, cloves, and nutmeg to a low boil, stirring occasionally. Add the baking soda and stir until the mixture foams up in the saucepan, 1 to 2 minutes.

4. Pour the hot molasses mixture over the butter and stir to melt the butter. Add the egg and stir to blend. Gradually stir in the flour, baking powder, and salt.

5. Turn the dough out onto a lightly floured surface and knead it lightly until the dough is smooth; form it into a ball. Using a lightly floured rolling pin, roll the dough out to a ¼-inch thickness.

6. Cut out the cookies using floured cookie cutters. Place the cookies on the prepared baking sheet, leaving 1 inch of space between them. Gather, reroll, and cut the scraps of dough.

7. Decorate the cookies with bits of the dried fruits. If you plan to string the cookies on ribbons for hanging, use a skewer or ice pick to make small holes at the tops. Bake the cookies for 13 to 15 minutes, or until crisp.

8. Let the cookies cool on the baking sheet for 2 to 3 minutes, then transfer them to a rack to cool completely.

9. Meanwhile, prepare the icing: In a small bowl, combine the confectioners' sugar, water, and vanilla, and stir until thick and smooth; set aside.

10. Fill a pastry bag with the icing and pipe it onto the cookies. Add details with more bits of the dried fruits, if desired.   *Makes about 2 dozen*

Gingerbread Cookies

SPRINGERLE

Springerle, anise-flavored cookies molded with decorative designs, are believed to have originated in Germany in the 17th or 18th century. The descendants of earlier molded cookies made from honey-sweetened dough or from marzipan, springerle were baked at holidays, and reached their height of popularity in the early 19th century.

The word *springerle,* from a southern German dialect, means to jump up, referring to the action of the dough, which doubles in height as the cookies bake. These extremely hard cookies were often decorated with colored-sugar mixtures, hung on a Christmas tree, and saved from year to year.

The making of springerle molds was an art in itself. The collection at left includes 19th-century examples as well as a new piece (with the large floral image).

The following recipe is adapted from a classic German-American springerle recipe published in 1856 by Wilhelm Vollmer in his *United States Cook Book.* To make sure your dough takes the sharpest design impression, you should use a true springerle mold or a springerle rolling pin and try pressing out a few cookies to perfect your technique.

SPRINGERLE COOKIES

4 eggs	2½ teaspoons aniseed
2 cups superfine sugar	About 5 cups flour
Grated zest of ½ lemon	Olive oil

1. About 30 minutes before making dough, place springerle molds in refrigerator to chill (chilled molds will help prevent dough from sticking). As you work with one mold, keep others in refrigerator.

2. To make dough, in large bowl beat eggs to a thick froth. Sift in sugar gradually, and beat until creamy. Add lemon zest and aniseed, then gradually fold in 3½ cups of the flour. Depending on type of flour used and the weather, dough may be too sticky. If this is the case, lightly flour work surface and place dough on it. Using your hands, work an additional ½ to 1½ cups flour into dough, being careful to add only enough to keep dough from sticking to rolling pin when it is rolled out.

3. Brush chilled springerle molds very lightly with olive oil, then wipe molds with cloth. If images are elaborate, dust molds lightly with flour.

4. Lightly flour work surface. Divide dough into thirds and roll out to ½-inch thickness. One at a time, press each mold into dough and gently pull it away. Cut cookies out along borders (true springerle cookies always have raised borders). Place them on ungreased baking sheets to dry for at least 12 hours, enabling imprinted design to set. (Dry cookies in unheated room or cool part of house to prevent them from cracking during baking.) If you wish to use cookies as decorations, pierce them with skewer at this time; be sure hole is not too small or it will close during baking.

5. To bake, preheat oven to 325°. Remove cookies from ungreased baking sheets; lightly grease sheets. Replace cookies on greased baking sheets and bake for 15 to 20 minutes, or until bottoms are golden brown (tops will remain pale).

Makes 5 to 6 dozen 2-inch cookies

Dream Bars

Even though this rich cookie has numerous variations, most recipes call for a buttery crust and a chewy topping of nuts and coconut. Perhaps the ultimate bar cookie, these should satisfy any cookie lover's dreams.

CRUST
1 cup flour
¼ cup (packed) dark brown sugar
1 stick (4 ounces) chilled butter, cut into pieces

COCONUT-PECAN TOPPING
1 cup sweetened shredded coconut
1 cup coarsely chopped pecans

2 tablespoons flour
¾ teaspoon baking powder
¼ teaspoon salt
2 eggs
¾ cup (packed) dark brown sugar
1 teaspoon vanilla extract
1 teaspoon grated lemon zest

1. Preheat the oven to 375°. Grease and flour an 11 x 7-inch baking pan.
2. Make the crust: In a medium bowl, stir together the flour and brown sugar. Using your fingers or a fork, mix in the butter until the mixture resembles very coarse crumbs. Press the mixture into the prepared pan and bake for 10 minutes.
3. Meanwhile, make the coconut-pecan topping: In a small bowl, combine the coconut, pecans, flour, baking powder, and salt.
4. In a medium bowl, beat together the eggs, brown sugar, vanilla, and lemon zest. Stir the dry ingredients into the egg mixture.
5. Remove the pan from the oven and let the crust cool slightly. Pour the coconut-pecan topping over the crust, spreading it evenly with a rubber spatula, and bake for another 18 to 20 minutes, or until the topping is golden brown and set.
6. Let cool slightly in the pan on a rack, then cut into 20 bars while still warm.

Makes 20

Benne Wafers

Benne (sesame seed) cookies have been a Southern specialty—particularly associated with Charleston, South Carolina—since the days when sesame seeds were brought over from Africa on slave ships. These thin, chewy wafers are loaded with toasted sesame seeds. Toasting the seeds, like toasting nuts, brings out their full flavor.

1 cup sesame seeds
¾ cup flour
¼ teaspoon baking powder
1 stick (4 ounces) butter, softened to
  room temperature

1 cup (packed) light brown sugar
1 egg
1 teaspoon vanilla extract

1. In an ungreased, heavy skillet, toast the sesame seeds over low heat, stirring constantly, until light golden, 5 to 7 minutes. Set aside to cool.

2. In a small bowl, stir together the flour and baking powder.

3. In a medium bowl, cream the butter and sugar. Beat in the egg. Beat in the dry ingredients, then add the toasted sesame seeds and the vanilla, and stir until combined.

4. Transfer the dough to a sheet of waxed paper or plastic wrap and shape it into a log about 1½ inches thick. Wrap the log of dough and refrigerate it overnight.

5. Preheat the oven to 350°. Grease a large baking sheet.

6. Using a very sharp knife, cut the dough into ⅛-inch-thick slices and place them on the prepared baking sheet, leaving 3 to 4 inches of space between them. Bake for 8 to 10 minutes, or until the edges are lightly browned.

7. Let the wafers cool for about 30 seconds on the baking sheet, then, using a thin metal spatula and wiping it clean periodically, transfer them to a rack to cool completely.

Makes about 6 dozen

Pecan Balls

Although a wonderful treat any time of the year, these dense, sugar-dusted cookies are traditionally baked at Christmas. They do make attractive holiday gifts, especially when placed in individual foil bonbon cups and set in decorative tins.

1½ cups pecan halves
1 stick (4 ounces) butter, softened to
*   room temperature*
¼ cup granulated sugar

2 teaspoons vanilla extract
2 cups flour
¼ cup confectioners' sugar

1. Preheat the oven to 300°. Lightly grease a baking sheet.

2. Place the pecans in an ungreased, heavy skillet. Toast them over medium-high heat, shaking the pan frequently, until golden brown, 5 to 8 minutes.

3. Process the pecans in a food processor or blender just until finely chopped; do not overprocess or the nuts will turn into an oily paste. Set aside.

4. In a large bowl, cream the butter and granulated sugar until light and fluffy. Beat in the vanilla. Beat in the chopped pecans. Gradually add the flour, beating until just incorporated. The dough will be firm and slightly crumbly.

5. Shape the dough into 1-inch balls and place them on the prepared baking sheet, leaving 1 inch of space between them. Bake for 18 to 20 minutes, or until the cookies just begin to brown around the sides. The tops should remain pale.

6. Let the cookies cool on the baking sheet for 5 minutes, then carefully transfer them to a rack. While they are still warm, sift the confectioners' sugar over them, then let them cool completely.

Makes about 3½ dozen

Pecan Lace Wafers

These crisp, filigreed lace cookies are so pretty, they practically create a party all by themselves. Make some of each type—wafers glazed with chocolate and rolled cones filled with whipped cream—and offer them on a tea tray. Or, serve the chocolate-glazed wafers with ice cream or sherbet in pretty, old-fashioned glass dishes. The cone-shaped, cream-filled cookies are delicious accompanied with raspberries or strawberries. Though not the easiest cookies to make, pecan lace wafers are worth the trouble. One helpful hint: be sure the baking sheet is cool before dropping the batter onto it.

While today we can buy nuts in many ready-to-use forms, this was not always so. Around the turn of the century, cooks relied on tips such as the following, from a popular household manual: "Pecan meats can be easily removed without breaking, by pouring boiling water over the nuts and letting them stand until cold. Then crack with a hammer, striking the small end of the pecan."

1 stick (4 ounces) butter, softened to room temperature
⅔ cup (packed) light brown sugar
½ cup light corn syrup
1 cup flour
1 cup finely chopped pecans
½ teaspoon vanilla extract

CHOCOLATE GLAZE
2 ounces semisweet chocolate
1 teaspoon vegetable shortening

WHIPPED CREAM FILLING
1 cup heavy cream
2 tablespoons confectioners' sugar

1. Preheat the oven to 375°. Lightly grease a baking sheet.

2. Cut the butter into 1-inch pieces. In a medium saucepan, heat the butter, brown sugar, and corn syrup over medium heat until the butter melts and the mixture comes to a boil. Remove the pan from the heat, add the flour, pecans, and vanilla extract, and stir until combined.

3. Using a teaspoonful of batter for each wafer, drop the batter onto the prepared baking sheet, leaving 3 inches of space between the wafers (bake no more than 9 at a time). Bake for 5 to 7 minutes, or until the wafers spread to about 2½ inches and the surface looks caramelized and lacy.

4. Let the wafers cool on the baking sheet for 20 to 30 seconds. To make cones, roll the wafers while they are still warm. (If the wafers cool before you have rolled them, return them to the oven for a moment to soften.) For flat cookies, transfer the wafers to a rack to cool completely.

5. Let the baking sheet cool, then make a second batch of wafers.

6. Meanwhile, make the chocolate glaze: In the top of a double boiler over hot, not simmering, water, melt the chocolate and vegetable shortening and stir until smooth; transfer the glaze to a bowl.

7. Drizzle the chocolate glaze from a spoon over the flat wafers, or carefully half-dip the wafers into the glaze. Dip just the edges of the cone-shaped wafers into the glaze.

8. Just before serving, make the filling: In a medium bowl, whip the cream with the confectioners' sugar until stiff. Spoon or pipe the sweetened whipped cream into the cone-shaped wafers. *Makes about 8 dozen*

Two-Tone Icebox Cookies

Two-Tone Icebox Cookies

If you're in a hurry, this cookie dough can be frozen for forty-five minutes instead of refrigerated for four hours before baking. Or, the dough can be frozen for up to three months, then thawed in the refrigerator overnight before shaping.

2 sticks (8 ounces) butter, softened to room temperature
1 cup sugar
1 egg plus 1 egg yolk
1 teaspoon vanilla extract

2¾ cups flour
2 tablespoons unsweetened cocoa powder
1 egg white, beaten (optional)
Chopped or sliced blanched almonds (optional)

1. In a large bowl, cream the butter and sugar. Beat in the egg and egg yolk, then beat in the vanilla. Gradually add the flour, beating just until incorporated.

2. Divide the dough into two equal portions. Beat the cocoa into one portion. Form the dough into two balls. Use one of the techniques that follow to shape the cookies, then proceed with the baking directions in Steps 3 and 4.

For log cookies: Roll both the light and dark dough into ½-inch-thick ropes and cut the ropes into 2-inch lengths. Dip each log into beaten egg white, then into chopped or sliced almonds.

For checkerboard cookies (see the step-by-step photographs, pages 98-99): Using the dark dough, form ⅝-inch-diameter ropes about 9 inches long; form light-dough ropes the same size. Working with four ropes (two of each color) at a time, place one dark and one light rope side by side and press together; then place the other two ropes on top so that light and dark alternate; press together lightly. Wrap the dough loosely in plastic wrap and refrigerate for at least 4 hours, or overnight. Repeat with the remaining ropes. Remove one roll of dough at a time from the refrigerator and use a sharp knife to cut it into ¼-inch-thick slices.

For pinwheel cookies (see the step-by-step photographs, pages 98-99): Divide each ball of dough into eight equal portions, then roll each out to a 6 x 5-inch rectangle. Place a dark piece of dough on top of a light one (or vice versa) and roll the two layers together tightly from one long side, like a jelly roll. Wrap each roll in plastic wrap and refrigerate for at least 4 hours. Use a sharp knife to cut the dough into ¼-inch-thick slices.

3. Preheat the oven to 350°. Lightly grease a baking sheet.

4. Place the cookies on the prepared baking sheet, leaving 1 inch of space between the cookies, and bake for 8 to 10 minutes for checkerboard or pinwheel cookies and 11 to 13 minutes for log cookies, or until they are lightly browned around the edges.

5. Cool the cookies on a rack.

Makes 8 to 12 dozen

DESIGNS FOR TWO-TONE ICEBOX COOKIES

CHECKERBOARD

Two-Tone Icebox Cookies can be designed in any number of ways. One of the simpler patterns is the checkerboard, which is formed by alternating ropes of light and dark dough. The size of the cookies can be varied by making the diameter of the ropes larger or smaller, but the cookies should not be sliced any thicker than ¼ inch. If desired, the cookie log can be patted into a slightly squarer shape.

Divide the light and dark portions of dough into eight pieces each. Roll each piece into a rope ⅝ inch in diameter and about 9 inches long, for a total of 16 ropes.

Working with four ropes (two of each color) at a time, press a light-dough rope and a dark-dough rope together. Repeat with the other two ropes.

BULL'S-EYE

To make bull's-eye cookies, wrap a dough rectangle of one color around a dough log of contrasting color. Make half the cookies with dark-dough centers and half with light-dough centers. If desired, you can use this same technique to give the checkerboard pattern (above) a border: simply roll out some of the dough to a rectangle ⅛ inch thick and big enough to wrap around the checkerboard cookie roll.

Divide the light and dark portions of dough into four pieces each. Roll two pieces of each color into 6 x 4-inch rectangles; roll two pieces of each color into 6-inch logs.

There should be two rectangles and two logs of each color. Place a log of dough about ½ inch in from the long side of a rectangle of dough of contrasting color.

PINWHEEL

To make pinwheel cookies, layer two rectangles of different-colored dough together, then roll them up. For a colorful variation on this theme, instead of using the chocolate and vanilla doughs shown here, add two different food colors to the plain dough: Try red-and-green pinwheels for Christmas. Or, for Halloween, use cocoa to make chocolate dough and color the other portion of dough a pale orange.

Divide the light and dark portions of dough into four pieces each, for a total of eight pieces. Roll each piece into a 6 x 5-inch rectangle about ⅛ inch thick.

Place one rectangle of dough on top of another rectangle of contrasting color. It doesn't matter which color is on top. There should be four pairs of rectangles.

Place one pair of ropes on top of the other, alternating light and dark doughs. Press the ropes together to form a long roll. Repeat with the remaining dough.

Wrap each cookie roll in plastic wrap and refrigerate for at least 4 hours, or overnight, to firm up. When ready to bake, slice the roll into ¼-inch-thick cookies.

To bake, place the cookies 1 inch apart on a lightly greased baking sheet and bake at 350° for 8 to 10 minutes, or until lightly browned around the edges.

Roll up the log in the rectangle of dough. Pinch the ends of the dough rectangle together to completely enclose the log and press the seam lightly to smooth it.

Wrap each cookie roll in plastic wrap and refrigerate for at least 4 hours, or overnight, to firm up. When ready to bake, slice the roll into ¼-inch-thick cookies.

To bake, place the cookies 1 inch apart on a lightly greased baking sheet and bake at 350° for 8 to 10 minutes, or until lightly browned around the edges.

Starting at one long side, tightly roll up the layered dough. Pinch the ends of the rectangles together to seal, then press lightly to smooth the seam against the log.

Wrap each cookie roll in plastic wrap and refrigerate for at least 4 hours, or overnight, to firm up. When ready to bake, slice the roll into ¼-inch-thick cookies.

To bake, place the cookies 1 inch apart on a lightly greased baking sheet and bake at 350° for 8 to 10 minutes, or until lightly browned around the edges.

Cranberry-Pecan Pie with Cornmeal Crust

Instead of pumpkin or mince pie, offer this colorful dessert at Thanksgiving or Christmas dinner, and top it off with a scoop of vanilla ice cream. The refreshingly tart filling, made by combining cranberries with fresh apples, dried apricots, pecans, and maple syrup, tastes like a crunchy cranberry relish. In fact, if the flour is omitted, the fruit and nut mixture can be served as a condiment with poultry or ham.

PASTRY
1 cup flour
⅓ cup yellow cornmeal
2 tablespoons sugar
¾ teaspoon salt
4 tablespoons chilled butter, cut into pieces
3 tablespoons chilled vegetable shortening, cut into pieces
4 to 5 tablespoons ice water

FILLING AND GLAZE
3 cups cranberries
2 medium Granny Smith or other tart green apples, unpeeled and finely chopped
¾ cup dried apricots, chopped
¾ cup chopped pecans
⅓ cup maple syrup
¼ cup flour
1 egg yolk beaten with 1 tablespoon milk
⅓ cup orange marmalade

1. Make the pastry: In a large bowl, combine the flour, cornmeal, sugar, and salt. With a pastry blender or two knives, cut in the butter and shortening until the mixture resembles coarse crumbs.

2. Sprinkle 2 tablespoons of the ice water over the mixture and toss it with a fork. The dough should be just barely moistened, enough so it will hold together when it is formed into a ball. If necessary, add up to 3 tablespoons more water, 1 tablespoon at a time. Form the dough into a flat disk, wrap in plastic wrap, and refrigerate for at least 30 minutes.

3. On a lightly floured surface, roll the dough out to a 12-inch circle. Fit the dough into a 9-inch glass pie plate. Trim the overhang to an even ½ inch and fold it under; crimp the dough to form a decorative border. Prick the pastry with a fork. Place the pie shell in the freezer to chill for at least 15 minutes before baking.

4. Preheat the oven to 400°.

5. Make the filling: In a food processor, pulsing the machine on and off, coarsely chop the cranberries. Transfer the cranberries to a large bowl, add the apples, apricots, pecans, maple syrup, and flour, and stir until well blended; set aside.

6. Line the pie shell with foil and fill it with pie weights or dried beans. Brush the pie border with the egg-yolk mixture and bake for 10 minutes. Remove the pie shell from the oven and reduce the oven temperature to 375°.

7. Remove the foil and weights from the pie shell and spoon the filling into the shell, spreading it evenly with a spatula. Return the pie to the oven and bake it for another 20 minutes, or until the crust is golden; set aside to cool slightly.

8. In a small saucepan, warm the marmalade over low heat until it is pourable. Spoon the warmed marmalade over the cranberry filling. *Makes one 9-inch pie*

Today, fresh whole cranberries are widely available in the fall. They can be put directly into the freezer until needed, or bought already frozen. In 1909, however, a household manual recommended that cooks take them "to a cool upstairs place and stir lightly with the hand occasionally, till dry; then leave them to freeze, as it happens, and they will keep both color and flavor as long as they last."

Bourbon-Pecan Pie

This Southern classic tastes especially good served with whipped cream flavored with bourbon and a small amount of sugar, or with run-raisin ice cream.

Pie Pastry (below)
4 tablespoons butter, softened to
room temperature
1/3 cup (packed) dark brown sugar

3 eggs
3/4 cup dark corn syrup
2 tablespoons bourbon
1 1/2 cups pecan halves

1. Make the Pie Pastry.
2. Preheat the oven to 350°.
3. In a mixing bowl, cream the butter and sugar. Add the eggs, one at a time, blending well after each addition. Beat in the corn syrup and bourbon until well blended. Stir in the pecans.
4. Pour the mixture into the pie shell and bake for 40 to 45 minutes, or until the filling has set and is slightly puffed. Cool the pies on a rack before serving.

Makes one 9-inch pie

Pie Pastry

Although the instructions given here are for making pie pastry by hand, it can also be made in a food processor. Just take care to process the ingredients very briefly, pulsing the machine on and off quickly; overprocessing will toughen the dough.

1 1/4 cups flour
3/4 teaspoon salt
4 tablespoons chilled butter, cut into pieces

3 tablespoons chilled vegetable shortening, cut into pieces
4 to 5 tablespoons ice water

1. In a large bowl, combine the flour and salt. With a pastry blender or two knives, cut in the butter and the shortening until the mixture resembles coarse crumbs.
2. Sprinkle 4 tablespoons of the ice water over the mixture and toss it with a fork. The dough should be moistened just enough so that it holds together when it is formed into a ball. If necessary, add up 1 tablespoon more water, drop by drop. Shape the dough into flat discs, warp in plastic wrap, and refrigerate for at least 30 minutes, or until well chilled.
3. On a lightly floured surface, roll the dough into a 12-inch circle. Fit the dough into a 9-inch pie pan. Trim the overhang to an even 1/2 inch all the way around. Fold the overhang over and crimp the dough to form a decorative border. Prick the pastry with a fork. Place the pie shell in the freezer for at least 15 minutes before filling and baking.

Makes one 9-inch crust

Pastry-Wrapped Pears

Frugal cooks have always saved pastry scraps (left after trimming a pie crust) to concoct homey treats like jam tarts and diminutive dumplings and turnovers. This elegant dessert, suitable for a holiday dinner or other festive meal, expands on the same theme. The pasty-wrapping technique could also be used with apples.

PASTRY	FILLING AND GLAZE
2½ cups flour	⅓ cup chopped walnuts
2 tablespoons sugar	¼ cup apricot preserves
1 teaspoon salt	½ teaspoon cinnamon
1 stick (4 ounces) chilled butter, cut into pieces	4 Bosc pears
5 tablespoons chilled vegetable	1 egg yolk
shortening, cut into pieces	1 tablespoon milk
8 tablespoons ice water	

1. Make the pastry: In a large bowl, combine the flour, sugar, and salt. With a pastry blender or two knives, cut in the butter and shortening until the mixture resembles coarse crumbs.

2. Sprinkle 4 tablespoons of the ice water over the mixture and toss it with a fork. The dough should be just barely moistened, enough so it will hold together when it is formed into a ball. If necessary, add up to 4 tablespoons more water, 1 tablespoon at a time. Divide the dough into 4 pieces, wrap each piece in plastic wrap, and refrigerate for at least 30 minutes.

3. On a lightly floured surface, roll out each piece of dough to a 12 x 10-inch rectangle. From each rectangle, cut a 10 x 10 x 10-inch triangle. Place the triangles on sheets of waxed paper. Cut 16 leaf shapes from the scraps, place them on waxed paper, and use a knife to mark veins on them. Cover the pastry triangles and leaves with plastic wrap and refrigerator them for at least 15 minutes before baking.

4. Meanwhile, make the filling: In a small bowl, stir together the walnuts, preserves, and cinnamon.

5. Without removing the stems, peel the pears. Carefully core each pear from the bottom to within ¾ inch of the stem end, then fill the cavities with the walnut mixture.

6. Line a baking sheet with baking parchment or foil. Lay the pastry triangles on the work surface. Moisten the edges of one triangle with water, then stand a pear in the center of the triangle. Bring the edges of the pastry together to enclose the pear, leaving the stem exposed, and pinch the edges together. Brush the backs of the pastry leaves with water and press them around the tops of the pastry-wrapped pears. Place the pears in the refrigerator for at least 15 minutes before baking.

7. Preheat the oven to 375°.

8. In a small bowl, stir together the egg yolk and milk. Brush the pastry with the egg glaze and bake for 20 to 25 minutes, or until the pastry is lightly browned. Serve the pastry-wrapped pears warm. *Makes 4 pastries*

Filbert Cake with Coffee Buttercream

In America, filberts, or hazelnuts, are grown mainly in the Pacific Northwest. Among the sweetest of nuts, they have long been recognized as a toothsome complement to chocolate. In this recipe, their delicious flavor blends particularly well with the coffee-flavored buttercream frosting. Be sure to use powdered instant coffee for the buttercream; instant coffee crystals may not dissolve completely.

CAKE
1 cup shelled filberts
2¾ cups sifted cake flour
2 teaspoons baking powder
¼ teaspoon salt
2 sticks (8 ounces) butter, softened to
　　room temperature
1½ cups sugar
3 eggs
1 cup sour cream
1 teaspoon vanilla extract

COFFEE BUTTERCREAM
¾ cup sugar
⅓ cup water
⅛ teaspoon cream of tartar
4 egg yolks
3 sticks (12 ounces) butter, softened to
　　room temperature and cut into
　　1-tablespoon pieces
2 teaspoons instant coffee powder,
　　preferably espresso
1 teaspoon vanilla extract

　　1. Make the cake: Preheat the oven to 375°. Butter the bottoms of two 8-inch round cake pans, then line them with circles of waxed paper. Butter and flour the waxed paper.

　　2. Place the filberts in a shallow baking pan and toast in the oven, stirring occasionally, until slightly browned, 5 to 10 minutes. Set aside to cool slightly. Reduce the oven temperature to 350°. Set aside 5 filberts for the garnish, and process the remaining filberts in a food processor just until finely ground; do not overprocess or the nuts will turn into a paste. Set aside.

　　3. In a medium bowl, stir together the flour, baking powder, and salt.

　　4. In a large bowl, cream the butter and sugar. Beat in the eggs, one at a time, beating well after each addition, then beat in the sour cream and vanilla. Gradually add the dry ingredients, beating well after each addition. Beat in the ground filberts.

　　5. Spread the batter evenly in the prepared pans. Rap the pans once or twice on the counter to remove any air pockets. Bake for 30 to 35 minutes, or until the cakes shrink from the sides of the pans and a toothpick inserted in the center of each cake comes out clean and dry. Let the cakes cool in the pans for 10 minutes, then turn them out onto racks to cool completely before frosting.

　　6. Meanwhile, make the buttercream: In a small, heavy saucepan, bring the sugar, water, and cream of tartar to a boil over medium-high heat. Reduce the heat to medium so that the mixture simmers, and cook, without stirring, until the sugar syrup registers exactly 238° on a candy thermometer, about 20 minutes.

　　7. In a medium bowl, beat the egg yolks until pale and lemon-colored. Slowly drizzle in the hot sugar syrup and beat constantly until cool, about 10 minutes.

　　8. Gradually beat in the butter, then the instant coffee and vanilla. Continue beating until the buttercream is uniform in color and just spreadable, about 3 minutes.

9. Assemble the cake: Remove the waxed paper from the layers. Set aside 1 cup of the buttercream for decoration, then spread a generous layer of buttercream over one cake layer. Top with the second layer, then spread a thin coat of buttercream over the top and sides of the cake. Refrigerate the cake for about 15 minutes to set the frosting, then spread a ¼-inch-thick layer of buttercream over the first coat. Fill a pastry bag with the reserved buttercream and pipe it decoratively on the cake. Garnish with the reserved filberts.

Makes one 8-inch layer cake

White Fruitcake

Fruitcake baking was traditionally a large-scale operation. *The Carolina Housewife,* published in 1847, included a recipe requiring twenty pounds each of butter, sugar, flour, and raisins; forty pounds of currants; twenty nutmegs; and twenty glasses each of wine and brandy. This more manageable recipe for a white fruitcake, with mostly light-colored fruit, makes six small loaves, which are perfect for holiday gifts. Bake each one in a separate foil pan, then wrap individually in festive seasonal papers.

2 cups golden raisins

1 cup chopped dried apricots

1 cup chopped mixed dried fruit

1 cup brandy

2 cups flour

2 teaspoons baking powder

1 teaspoon salt

2 sticks (8 ounces) butter

1 cup sugar

8 eggs

2 cups slivered blanched almonds

2 teaspoons grated lemon zest

2 teaspoons vanilla extract

6 tablespoons bourbon

1. In a medium bowl, combine the raisins, apricots, and dried fruit, and pour the brandy over them. Set aside to soak for at least 4 hours, or overnight.

2. Preheat the oven to 325°. Butter six 5½ x 3 x 2-inch mini loaf pans.

3. In a small bowl, stir together the flour, baking powder, and salt; set aside.

4. In a large bowl, cream the butter and sugar. Beat in the eggs, one at a time. Alternating among the three, stir in the dry ingredients, the fruit-brandy mixture, and the almonds, beating well after each addition. Blend in the lemon zest and vanilla.

5. Divide the batter evenly among the prepared pans (they will be nearly full). Rap the pans once or twice on the counter to remove any air pockets. (For easier handling, place the pans on a large baking sheet.) Bake for 45 to 50 minutes, or until the cakes shrink from the sides of the pans and a toothpick inserted in the center of each cake comes out clean and dry.

6. Let the cakes cool in the pans on racks for 30 minutes, then turn them out to cool completely.

7. Pour 1 tablespoon of bourbon over each cake and let stand for at least 4 hours. If not serving immediately, wrap each cake in a bourbon-soaked cheesecloth, then in plastic wrap, and store in a tightly closed container for up to 3 months. The cakes may also be frozen for up to 4 months.

Makes 6 mini loaves

ELEGANT TRUFFLES

Truffles are not hard to make, but the chocolate can get soft and sticky when you are working with it, so be sure that your kitchen is not excessively hot—and work quickly. The finished truffles should be stored in the refrigerator, between layers of wax paper in an airtight container. If you cover the container with plastic wrap and then with foil, the sweets will keep for up to two weeks in the refrigerator or two months in the freezer. To defrost, thaw overnight in the refrigerator.

BASIC CHOCOLATE TRUFFLES

½ cup heavy cream
¼ cup unsalted butter
Pinch salt
8 ounces semisweet or bittersweet chocolate, in pieces
1 teaspoon vanilla extract

2 tablespoons unsweetened cocoa powder
2 tablespoons confectioners' sugar, plus additional for coating

1. In small saucepan, warm cream, butter, and salt over low heat just until butter is melted.

2. Stir in chocolate. Reduce heat to very low and cook, stirring, until chocolate is melted and smooth. Remove from heat and stir in vanilla. Pour mixture into medium bowl, cover with plastic wrap, and refrigerate until firm, about 3 hours.

3. Shape and coat truffles: In small bowl, mix together cocoa and 2 tablespoons of the confectioners' sugar. Place bowl of chocolate in larger bowl of ice and water to keep mixture firm. Using melon baller or 2 teaspoons, dipped in confectioners' sugar, scoop some chilled chocolate into small ball. Roll ball in cocoa-sugar mixture. (You can also sprinkle your fingers and palms with confectioners' sugar and shape mixture by hand, but work quickly to keep chocolate from melting.)

4. After coating each truffle, place in small fluted paper candy cup and keep refrigerated. Let truffles stand at room temperature for 10 to 15 minutes before serving; do not let them remain at room temperature for very long or they will become too soft.   Makes 4 dozen

Flavor variations: You can alter the basic truffle recipe above by adding flavorings such as these:

◆ Rum Raisin: Into the melted chocolate, stir ¼ cup chopped golden raisins that have been soaked for 30 minutes in ¼ cup warmed dark rum and then drained. You can also stir in the rum if you like.
◆ Coffee Kahlua: Stir ¼ cup Kahlua and 1 tablespoon instant espresso powder into the cream and melted butter before adding the chocolate.
◆ Orange: Stir 1 tablespoon grated orange zest and ½ teaspoon orange extract into the melted chocolate.

Coating variations: In addition to flavoring the truffles, try rolling them in any of the following: toasted flaked coconut; chopped almonds or pistachios; plain granulated sugar, or ¾ cup granulated sugar tossed with 2 teaspoons grated orange zest that has been patted dry.

Kentucky Bourbon Cake

Many old recipes for pound cake include brandy, but the cook who first substituted bourbon whiskey created a Kentucky classic. Mace, which is derived from the outer covering of the nutmeg kernel, is another traditional flavoring for pound cake. If it is not readily available, ground nutmeg makes an acceptable substitute.

2 cups raisins

½ cup bourbon

2 cups flour

1 teaspoon ground mace or nutmeg

¾ teaspoon baking soda

¼ teaspoon salt

1½ sticks (6 ounces) butter, softened to room temperature

½ cup (packed) dark brown sugar

½ cup granulated sugar

4 eggs

½ cup molasses

1 teaspoon vanilla extract

2 cups chopped pecans, plus ¾ cup pecan halves

1. Preheat the oven to 350°. Butter a 10-inch tube pan and line the bottom with a ring of waxed paper. Butter the waxed paper.

2. Place the raisins in a small bowl and pour ¼ cup of the bourbon over them. Set aside to soak for at least 1 hour, stirring occasionally. Reserving the bourbon, drain the raisins; set aside.

3. In a small bowl, stir together the flour, mace, baking soda, and salt.

4. In a large bowl, cream the butter and the brown and granulated sugars. Add the eggs, one at a time, beating well after each addition. Add the molasses, vanilla, and the bourbon used to soak the raisins.

5. Gradually add the dry ingredients, beating well after each addition. Fold in the chopped pecans and the drained raisins.

6. Spread the batter evenly in the prepared pan. Rap the pan once or twice on the counter to remove any air pockets. Arrange the pecans halves decoratively on top of the batter and bake for 50 to 55 minutes, or until the cake shrinks from the sides of the pan and a toothpick inserted in the center of the cake comes out clean and dry.

7. Let the cake cool in the pan for 30 minutes. Turn the cake out onto a plate and remove the waxed paper. Then invert the cake onto a rack, right-side up, to cool completely.

8. Place the cake in an airtight container and drape a sheet of cheesecloth over the cake. Slowly pour the remaining ¼ cup bourbon over the cloth and cake, close the container tightly, and store for up to 3 months.   *Makes one 10-inch tube cake*

Orange-Chocolate Cake

Here is a cake that will delight those who like their chocolate desserts intensely rich. The velvety frosting is a form of ganache, a confectioner's mixture (often used to make truffles) consisting basically of melted chocolate and cream. Since the recipe calls for nine ounces of chocolate, be sure to use a good-quality product. Experiment with different brands of semisweet and bittersweet chocolate: European brands labeled "extra-bittersweet" are particularly recommended. Marmalades also vary in sweetness; consider trying one of the sharp-flavored English brands, or else one that is prepared with ginger or whiskey.

CAKE

2 cups flour

½ cup unsweetened cocoa powder

1 teaspoon baking powder

¼ teaspoon baking soda

¼ teaspoon salt

1 stick (4 ounces) butter, softened to
   room temperature

1⅓ cups sugar

3 eggs

⅔ cup buttermilk

1 tablespoon grated orange zest

½ teaspoon orange extract

FROSTING AND FILLING

9 ounces semisweet chocolate

1¼ cups sour cream

2 tablespoons confectioners' sugar

½ teaspoon orange extract

½ cup orange marmalade

1. Make the cake: Preheat the oven to 350°. Butter two 8-inch round cake pans and line the bottoms with circles of waxed paper. Butter the waxed paper, then flour the pans.

2. In a small bowl, stir together the flour, cocoa, baking powder, baking soda, and salt.

3. In a large bowl, cream the butter and sugar. Beat in the eggs, one at a time, beating well after each addition. Beat in the buttermilk, orange zest, and orange extract. Add the dry ingredients and beat just until blended; do not overbeat.

4. Spread the batter evenly in the prepared pans. Rap the pans once or twice on the counter to remove any air pockets. Bake for 25 to 30 minutes, or until the cakes shrink from the sides of the pans and a toothpick inserted in the center of each cake comes out clean and dry. Let the cakes cool in the pans for 10 minutes, then turn them out onto racks to cool completely before frosting and filling.

5. Meanwhile, make the frosting: Cut the chocolate into large pieces. In the top of a double boiler over hot, not simmering, water, melt the chocolate, stirring until smooth. Set aside to cool slightly. Stir in the sour cream, confectioners' sugar, and orange extract, and continue stirring until smooth; set aside.

6. For the filling, place the marmalade in a small saucepan and warm it over low heat until it is spreadable.

7. Assemble the cake: Remove the waxed paper from the layers. Spread the marmalade over one cake layer. Top with the second layer, then frost the top and sides of the cake with the chocolate mixture.   *Makes one 8-inch layer cake*

Raspberry Cheesecake

Although it has become an American restaurant mainstay, cheesecake originated in Europe. Martha Washington's recipe, recorded in the handwritten family cookbook she inherited, called for "new milk" and rennet (added to turn the milk into cheese), butter, cream, sugar, currants, rosewater, and nutmeg.

1 package (8½ ounces) chocolate wafers
⅓ cup butter, melted
2 packages (8 ounces each) cream cheese,
*   softened to room temperature*
¾ cup sugar
1 tablespoon flour

1 cup sour cream
3 eggs
3 tablespoons lemon juice, preferably fresh
2 teaspoons vanilla extract
¼ cup seedless raspberry jam
½ pint fresh raspberries

1. Preheat the oven to 350°.

2. Make the crust: In a food processor or blender, process the chocolate wafers to fine crumbs; transfer the crumbs to a bowl. Add the melted butter and stir to combine, then pat the crumb mixture into the bottom and halfway up the sides of an 8½-inch springform pan; set aside.

3. Make the filling: In a medium bowl, beat the cream cheese and sugar until smooth. Beat in the flour, then the sour cream. Beat in the eggs, one at a time, beating well after each addition.

4. Add the lemon juice and vanilla, and beat until smooth. Pour the filling into the crust (the filling will rise above the crust). Bake for 1 hour to 1 hour and 10 minutes, or until the filling is set. Let the cake cool completely in the pan on a rack.

5. To serve, place the pan on a serving platter and remove the rim of the pan. Warm the jam in a small saucepan over low heat just until it is pourable. Arrange the raspberries decoratively on top of the cake and spoon the jam over them.

Makes one 8½-inch cake

Apple-Filled Crisscross

The filling of these latticed loaves is reminiscent of apple strudel, but the rich sour-cream dough is much easier to work with than fragile, paper-thin strudel dough. For ease in shaping the loaves, the strips of dough are simply crisscrossed, not braided, over the chunky apple-raisin-walnut filling.

PASTRY
1/4 cup lukewarm (105° to 115°) water
1 package active dry yeast
1/4 cup granulated sugar
1/3 cup sour cream, at room temperature
2 tablespoons lukewarm (105° to 115°) milk
1 egg, lightly beaten
1 teaspoon grated lemon zest
1/2 teaspoon vanilla extract
About 3 cups flour
1/4 teaspoon salt
6 tablespoons butter, softened to room
    temperature

FILLING
1 small apple, such as Granny Smith or
    Golden Delicious, unpeeled and
    coarsely chopped

1/4 cup raisins
3 tablespoons coarse fresh breadcrumbs
1/4 cup coarsely chopped walnuts
2 tablespoons sugar
1/2 teaspoon cinnamon
1/4 teaspoon grated lemon zest
1 teaspoon lemon juice

EGG GLAZE
1 egg yolk
1 tablespoon milk

ICING
1 cup confectioners' sugar
2 tablespoons lemon juice

Northern Spy, Newtown Pippin, Sweet Bough, Black Twig, Jonathan, Twenty Ounce, Wealthy, Winesap, Roxbury Russet, Grimes Golden—the names of America's old apple varieties form a sweet poetry all their own. More and more growers around the country are devoting their efforts to preserving "antique" fruit varieties. Look for old-fashioned apples at farm markets and orchard stands; sample their varied flavors and textures, and ask about their best uses.

1. Make the pastry: Place the water in a small bowl and sprinkle the yeast over it. Stir in a large pinch of granulated sugar and let the mixture stand until the yeast begins to foam, about 5 minutes.

2. In a small bowl, stir together the remaining granulated sugar, the sour cream, milk, egg, lemon zest, and vanilla; set aside.

3. In a large bowl, stir together 2½ cups of flour and the salt, and make a well in the center. Pour in the yeast mixture and the milk mixture, and stir until the mixture forms a soft dough.

4. Add the butter and mix until well combined. Transfer the dough to a lightly floured surface and knead it until smooth and elastic, about 10 minutes, adding up to ½ cup more flour if necessary. Form the dough into a ball and place it in a large greased bowl. Cover the bowl with a slightly dampened kitchen towel, set aside in a warm, draft-free place, and let the dough rise until it doubles in bulk, 45 minutes to 1 hour.

5. Meanwhile, make the filling: In a medium bowl, stir together the chopped apple, raisins, breadcrumbs, nuts, granulated sugar, cinnamon, lemon zest, and lemon juice; set aside.

6. Grease and flour two baking sheets.

7. Punch the dough down, then transfer it to a lightly floured surface and knead it for about 5 minutes.

Apple-Filled Crisscross

8. Using a lightly floured rolling pin, roll out the dough to an 18 x 8-inch rectangle, then cut it into two 9 x 8-inch rectangles. Place each rectangle of dough on a prepared baking sheet.

9. Spread half of the apple filling in a 2-inch-wide strip down the center of each piece of dough, leaving a border of about $\frac{1}{2}$ inch at the top and bottom. Starting $\frac{1}{2}$ inch from the filling, make diagonal cuts $\frac{1}{2}$ inch apart, from the filling out to the edges of the dough, on both sides. Crisscross the strips over the filling. Tuck the last two strips under and press firmly to seal them.

10. Set the loaves aside, uncovered, in a warm, draft-free place and let the dough rise for 20 to 25 minutes, or until almost doubled in bulk.

11. Preheat the oven to 375°.

12. Make the egg glaze: In a small bowl, stir together the egg yolk and milk.

13. Brush one loaf with half of the egg glaze and bake for 15 to 17 minutes, or until golden brown. (Leave the second loaf in the refrigerator or until ready to bake, but no longer than 1 hour.)

14. Transfer the baked loaf to a rack to cool. Meanwhile, glaze and bake the second loaf.

15. Make the icing: In a medium bowl, stir together the confectioners' sugar and lemon juice until smooth and pourable; add a few drops more lemon juice, if necessary. Drizzle the icing over both loaves while still warm.

Makes two 9-inch loaves

Cranberry-Almond Bread

2 cups flour
³/₄ cups sugar
2 teaspoons baking powder
¹/₂ teaspoon salt
³/₄ cup milk
6 tablespoons butter, melted

1 egg, slightly beaten
1 tablespoon grated orange zest
1 teaspoon almond extract
1 cup fresh or frozen cranberries
1 cup sliced almonds

1. Preheat the oven to 325°. Butter a 9 x 5-inch loaf pan.

2. In a large bowl, blend the flour, sugar, baking powder, and salt. In another bowl, combine the milk, melted butter, egg, orange zest, and almond extract. Add the wet ingredients to the dry ingredients and stir just until no streaks of flour remain. Fold in the cranberries and almonds.

3. Pour the batter into the prepared loaf pan and spread evenly. Bang the pan once or twice on the counter to remove any air pockets. Bake for 1 hour and 10 minutes, or until the top is golden and a toothpick inserted in the center of the bread comes out clean. Cool the bread in the pan for 10 minutes and then turn it out onto a rack to cool completely before slicing.

Makes 1 loaf

Dark Gingerbread

2 cups flour
1 tablespoon unsweetened cocoa
  powder
1 ¹/₂ teaspoons baking soda
2 ¹/₂ teaspoons ground ginger
¹/₂ teaspoon allspice
¹/₄ teaspoon salt

²/₃ cup molasses
²/₃ cup sour cream
1 stick (4 ounces) butter, softened to
  room temperature
¹/₂ cup (packed) dark brown sugar
2 eggs, lightly beaten

1. Preheat the oven to 350°. Butter and flour a 9 x 9-inch baking pan.

2. In a small bowl, stir together the flour, cocoa, baking soda, ginger, allspice, and salt. In another small bowl, stir together the molasses and sour cream.

3. In a large bowl, cream the butter and sugar until smooth. Add the eggs and beat until blended. Alternating between the two, add the dry ingredients and the molasses mixture, beating well after each addition.

4. Spread the batter evenly in the prepared pan. Rap the pan once or twice on the counter to remove any air pockets. Bake for 30 to 35 minutes, or until the cake shrinks from the sides of the pan and a toothpick inserted in the center of the gingerbread comes out clean and dry.

5. Let the gingerbread cool in the pan on a rack, then cut it into squares and serve warm, or at room temperature.

Makes one 9-inch square cake

Sweet Potato Swirl Bread

This colorful bread is laced with dark swirls of cocoa, a pleasant counterpoint to the sweetness of the potatoes. Whenever you have leftover sweet potatoes—perhaps after a big holiday meal—this is a delicious and novel way to use them. In cooking potatoes specifically for this recipe, you have several options. Slow baking is the method that brings out their flavor best; it seems to caramelize their natural sugar. However, if you're pressed for time, either cut the sweet potatoes into large chunks and steam them, or pierce the whole potatoes a few times with a fork and microwave them at 100% (high) power for 5 to 8 minutes.

1¾ cups flour
1 teaspoon baking soda
Pinch of salt
1 stick (4 ounces) butter, softened to
    room temperature
1 cup (packed) light brown sugar
2 eggs

1 teaspoon vanilla extract
1½ cups cooked, peeled, and mashed sweet
    potatoes (about 2 medium, 2¾ pounds
    total)
1 cup coarsely chopped walnuts
⅓ cup unsweetened cocoa powder

1. Preheat the oven to 350°. Butter and flour a 9 x 5-inch loaf pan.

2. In a small bowl, stir together the flour, baking soda, and salt; set aside.

3. In a medium bowl, cream the butter and sugar. Beat in the eggs one at a time, beating well after each addition, then beat in the vanilla. Stir in the sweet potatoes until thoroughly combined, then gradually add the dry ingredients, beating just until incorporated; do not overbeat. Stir in the walnuts.

4. Transfer one-third of the batter (about 1½ cups) to a small bowl, add the cocoa powder, and stir until well blended.

5. Spread the plain batter in the prepared pan, then spread the cocoa batter on top. Swirl a table knife through the batter to marbleize it. Rap the pan once or twice on the counter to remove any air pockets.

6. Bake for 1 hour to 1 hour and 10 minutes, or until the bread shrinks from the sides of the pan and a toothpick inserted in the center of the loaf comes out clean and dry.

7. Let the loaf cool in the pan on a rack, then turn it out to cool completely before slicing.

Makes one 9-inch loaf

The Carolina Housewife by a Lady of Charleston was published in 1847. Sarah Rutledge, who compiled the book, apparently knew her potatoes, both white and sweet. "Among the various ways of dressing sweet potatoes," she wrote, "that which appears the most generally preferred, is to bake them twice . . . . This way of baking twice, makes them more candied."

FANCY WRAPS FOR GIFTS FROM THE KITCHEN

Christmas is the season when home cooks and bakers indulge family and friends with special treats from the kitchen. Homemade specialties and fancy foods make wonderful gifts. After the last cookie is long gone, a clever gift container can be a useful and lasting reminder of your thoughtfulness.

Inexpensive glass jars come in a broad range of sizes and shapes. Here, wrapping paper is decoupaged onto a square canister jar to add interest to an otherwise simple container. A festive ribbon completes the presentation. Ribbons, papers, paints, and pressed flowers are only a few of the many materials that can be used. Handmade papers and artwork from greeting cards can be layered and then decoupaged onto jars, as done onto the clamp top "cherry" canister jar.

Baskets make marvelous gift containers and can be used again for any number of purposes. Present a classic combo of cookies and milk in a colorful holiday basket.

Terra-cotta flowerpots make creative containers for various items and are ideal for bread baking. Decorate with classic holiday designs or the recipient's favorite motif, using enamel glass paints. Or, use white transfer paper to paint a holiday bread recipe on the pot. Then include a bread mix for a quick treat.

Crafting a Country Christmas

Creating Your Own Christmas Treasures and Heirlooms

Perhaps because it reflects the personal sentiments of the crafter, nothing quite delights the heart so much as a hand-crafted gift or decoration. Whether an heirloom passed from generation to generation or a recent creation, these expressions of the spirit of the season will surely be the most cherished.

For those who want to create a very personal holiday, this chapter provides step-by-step instructions and clever ideas for a variety of decorative gifts and accessories. No Christmas would be complete without a welcoming wreath, or stockings hung by the fireside. And every home should have at least one pretty kissing ball hanging from a bright ribbon, or papier-mâché reindeer basking in the warm glow of Christmas candles. Adorn the tree with new, old-fashioned-style ornaments and whimsical garlands. Ribbon-decked baskets of fresh greens with gilded botanicals, and bowls of spicy orange pomanders, convey the fragrant scents of Christmas throughout the house. And as you entertain family and friends, the beautiful rubber-stamped serving tray will be a handy new addition to your Christmas accessories. Ideal as gifts or for personal use, these homemade treasures will give pleasure for years to come.

An array of homemade crafts lends a warm, personal touch to holiday decorating.

AN OUTDOOR WREATH

Trimming a wreath is a satisfying way to herald the holidays, and it can also be surprisingly easy. To make the striking wreath opposite, designed for outdoor use, you start with a ready-made evergreen wreath. After a decorative French horn is wired on, the wreath is embellished with a loose bow looped from upholstery cording, gold-painted leaves and pinecones, and an assortment of fresh berries, greens, apples, and miniature pineapples (all of which will last for several weeks in a cold climate). To judge the balance and design, hang the wreath up after you have attached the horn; you can adjust the trimmings, which are wired to florist's picks, and vary the number you use as you like. The materials are available at florists and at Christmas shops.

A. The ends of two pieces of florist's wire are twisted together to make a secure loop for hanging the wreath.

MATERIALS AND EQUIPMENT

· Ready-made fresh evergreen wreath ·
(wreath shown is about 2 feet in diameter)
· Sprigs of holly, seasonal greens, and berries · Magnolia leaves ·
· Pinecones · Miniature pineapples · Green apples ·
· Decorative French horn ·
· Upholstery cording, 4 yards each in red and gold ·
· Gold spray paint · Wooden florist's picks, 6 inches long ·
· Florist's wire · Small pruning shears ·
· Wire cutters · Scissors ·

◆

DIRECTIONS

1. To form a loop for hanging, use the wire cutters to cut two pieces of the florist's wire, each about 18 inches long. Holding the pieces together, shape them into a large "U" and pass it from front to back through the wreath. Twist the pieces together, tightening the wire against the greens, then twist the ends to make a loop (Illustration A).

2. Using the pruning shears, trim the sprigs and leaves as necessary. Wire a florist's pick (which comes with wire attached) to the stem or base of each sprig and pinecone, twisting the pick to secure (Illustration B).

3. Spray-paint the magnolia leaves and pinecones gold.

4. Place the French horn on the wreath, securing it in several places with florist's wire. Hang the wreath by the wire loop.

5. Hold the two pieces of cording together, knot them at each end, and tie them into a loose bow. Wire the bow to a florist's pick and poke it into the wreath near the top.

6. Arrange the holly, seasonal greens, and berries around the wreath, inserting the picks securely, then add the magnolia leaves and pinecones.

7. Push each apple and pineapple onto the blunt end of a florist's pick. Place the pineapples on the wreath and secure with florist's wire. Place the apples on the wreath (Illustration C).

B. Individual trimmings are wired onto florist's picks so that they can be easily arranged on the wreath.

C. Secured to florist's picks, the fruits are added after the leaves, greens, and berries have been attached.

AN INDOOR WREATH

Old-fashioned ornaments recall the spirit of Christmas Past on this pretty wreath. The Victorian paper cutouts are combined here with "tussie-mussies," or small nosegays, which are easy to make from doilies and miniature Christmas balls. To judge the balance and design, hang the wreath up before you add the trimmings; you can adjust the decorations and vary the number you use as you like. The materials are available at florists, novelty stores, and Christmas shops.

A. After the ribbon is wrapped around the wreath, the ends are overlapped and pinned at the top to secure them.

MATERIALS AND EQUIPMENT

· Ready-made fresh evergreen wreath ·
(wreath shown is about 2 feet in diameter)

· About 6 yards wire-edged ribbon, 2 inches wide ·

· Paper ornaments · Miniature glass Christmas balls on wires ·

· Circular paper doilies, 6 inches in diameter ·

· Wooden florist's picks, 6 inches long · Florist's wire ·

· Dressmaker's pins · Pushpins · Wire cutters ·

· Scissors ·

◆

DIRECTIONS

1. To form a loop for hanging, use the wire cutters to cut two pieces of the florist's wire, each about 18 inches long. Holding the pieces together, shape them into a large "U" and pass it from front to back through the wreath. Twist the pieces together, tightening the wire against the greens, then twist the ends to make a loop.

2. Wrap the ribbon around the wreath clockwise, beginning at the top front of the wreath and leaving a 2-inch tail; trim so there is a 1-inch overlap on the back. Secure the ends with one or two dressmaker's pins (Illustration A). Hang the wreath by the wire loop.

3. Make about a dozen tussie-mussies. For each, hold four Christmas balls together and insert their wires through the center of a doily; pinch the doily and twist it to gather it around the balls. Using the wire cutters, trim the wires 2 inches below the doily (Illustration B). Wire a florist's pick (which comes with wire attached) to the bottom of each tussie-mussie, twisting the pick to secure.

4. Cut a 1-yard length of ribbon; pull it through the center of the wreath at the top and align the ends to make a loop. Using a pushpin, temporarily pin the ends out of the way above the wreath. Make a generous bow from lengths of the remaining ribbon, using florist's wire or dressmaker's pins to secure the loops and soft center puff.

5. Arrange the tussie-mussies on the wreath, inserting the florist's picks to secure. Add the ornaments, tucking some into the greenery.

6. Hold the bow over the ribbon hanging loop to see where it looks best. Reposition the pushpin to secure the hanging loop at this point, then cut any excess ribbon above the pushpin. Place the bow over the pushpin and secure with a dressmaker's pin (Illustration C).

B. The tussie-mussies are made from glass balls and paper doilies, then wired onto florist's picks for easy arranging.

C. The wreath is hung by a sturdy wire loop camouflaged by ribbon; a decorative bow is added last.

COUNTRY CHRISTMAS WREATH

Plain or fancy, Christmas wreaths are a holiday tradition that can be personalized to suit any decor or taste. This everlasting wreath uses two distinctive ornaments, the deer and the Santa, to create dramatic focal points among the simple wooden shapes and natural materials, while the red bows add a cheerful color accent. The wooden ornaments are given a charming rustic appearance with crackle-painting techniques. Although the evergreens are silk and have no aroma, this wreath is festively scented with cinnamon sticks and pepper berries. To judge the balance and design, hang the wreath before you add the trimmings; you can adjust the decorations and vary their number as you like. The materials are available at florist's, craft, and fabric stores.

MATERIALS AND EQUIPMENT

· Grapevine wreath, 27 inches diameter · Silk pine garland, 6 feet long ·
· Bead garland, 6 feet long · 10 Holly berry picks · 16½ feet Red fiber mesh ribbon, 1½ inches wide ·
· 17 Cinnamon sticks, 12 inches long · Carved wooden ornaments: bird, 5 inches tall; 3 trees, 2½ inches tall ·
· Wooden ornaments: bear, 4½ inches tall; bird, 3 inches tall; deer, 6½ inches tall x 7½ inches;
moon, 3½ inches tall; Santa, 6 inches tall; 5 stars, 2 inches tall; 9 trees, 3 inches tall ·
· 3 Wooden flowerpots, 2 inches diameter · Antique medium, dark brown ·
· Blue, green, off-white, red, and yellow acrylic paints · Crackle medium · 10 Large pinecones ·
· Gold-leaf adhesive · Copper leafing · Patina-aging solution, rust · Pepper berries ·
· 20 Miniature pine cones · Green floral moss · Spool floral wire, 14 gauge ·
· 18 inches Floral wire, 20 gauge · Glue gun with glue sticks ·
· Paintbrushes · Needle-nose pliers · Scissors · Wire cutters ·

A. Drape the bead garland around the pine garland and hot-glue to secure.

B. Make three loops and secure with wire for the ribbon garland.

C. Hot-glue pinecones, ornaments, and other embellishments in place.

D. Place largest ornament over large bow and hot-glue in place.

DIRECTIONS

1. Wrap the pine garland around the wreath five or six times. Using pliers, secure with 14-gauge wire.

2. Drape the beaded garland around and through the pine garland. Hot-glue the beaded garland to secure in place (Illustration A).

3. Arrange the holly picks and hot-glue in place. Clip off the wire ends with wire cutters.

4. Using ribbon and starting 20 inches from one end, make three loops. Wrap 14-gauge wire around the base of the ribbon loops and secure (Illustration B). Repeat, making six additional sets of loops to create a bow garland. Leaving a 20-inch length, cut the ribbon. Loop the remaining ribbon into a large bow. Arrange the bow garland on the wreath and hot-glue the bows in place. Hot-glue the large bow to the bottom center of the wreath.

5. Break each cinnamon stick into two or three pieces. Hot-glue them inside the ribbon loops.

6. Paint the ornaments and pots with a base coat as desired. Let dry. Note: The color of the base coat will be visible through the crackle medium.

7. Using the crackle medium, generously paint the ornaments and pots. Set aside two to four hours until thoroughly dry.

8. Paint the ornaments and pots with the off-white paint. As the paint dries, cracks will appear. Paint the ornaments and pots with the antique medium, and wipe off the excess.

9. Using an old paintbrush, apply gold-leaf adhesive on the large pine cones. Set aside for one hour.

10. Using an old paintbrush, apply the copper leafing to the inside edges of the pine cones. Apply the rust patina over the copper leaf. Set aside until the copper leafing turns yellow and green.

11. Arrange the pine cones randomly on the wreath and hot-glue in place (Illustration C).

12. Hot-glue the ornaments and pots to the wreath, reserving the largest ornament. Hot-glue the largest ornament to the bottom center of the wreath above the large bow (Illustration D). Note: The large ornament may need support until the glue cools.

13. Hot-glue the miniature pine cones, pepper berries, and green floral moss to fill in any open spaces.

14. Form a loop for hanging using 20-gauge wire and needle-nose pliers.

THE GOLDEN TOUCH

A. Wear rubber gloves when applying the gold paint. Use mineral spirits for any necessary cleanup.

B. A pair of tweezers or needlenose pliers is useful for holding the items when dipping them.

C. If the gilded items slip through the boughs, secure them to the branches with fine wire.

A gold-painted basket filled with pine boughs and gilded natural objects—its handle wrapped with glossy ribbon tied in a generous bow—makes a lavish statement in an entranceway or on a dining table. This basket is filled with pine cones, Brazil nuts, almonds, walnuts, hazelnuts, pomegranates, artificial berries, and fabric leaves. Gilded seed pods, gourds, dried natural leaves, or artificial flowers would also work well. The basket and most of its contents can be stored away and brought out as an annual holiday tradition when the season commences. Only the greens will need to be replaced from year to year.

It is an easy task to transform the basket and accessories with a coat of gold paint. A splint basket in a simple shape offers a receptive surface to paint applied with a brush or a foam applicator. However, spray paint will be more effective in covering the intricate weaving of a wicker basket.

The pine cones, nuts, pomegranates, fabric leaves, and sprigs of artificial berries can be either dipped into or brushed with the paint. An old cake cooling rack, placed over newspaper to catch the drips, is a good surface on which to dry them; a piece of wire mesh or screening—or a sheet of waxed paper—would also serve the purpose.

MATERIALS

· Large unfinished basket · 1 quart gold paint ·
· Large and small pine cones ·
· Sprays of artificial berries · Unshelled nuts · Pomegranates ·
· Artificial ivy and leaves · Pine boughs or other evergreens ·
· Ribbon · Green tissue paper (optional) ·
· Small disposable foam paint applicators · Tweezers or pliers ·
· Cooling racks or waxed paper ·

◆

DIRECTIONS

1. Working in a well-ventilated area, cover the basket, inside and out, with gold paint (Illustration A). Set the basket aside to dry.

2. Using tweezers or pliers, dip the pine cones, berry sprays, and nuts into the gold paint (Illustration B). Set aside to dry on the cooling racks placed over newspaper, or on waxed paper.

3. Using a disposable foam paint applicator, paint the pomegranates, ivy, and other leaves; set aside to dry.

4. Twine the painted ivy around the edge of the basket. Place the pine boughs in the basket and arrange the pine cones, nuts, berries, and pomegranates on top of them (Illustration C). If the basket is very deep, fill the bottom with crumpled green tissue paper, then place the pine boughs on top of it.

5. Wrap the handle of the basket with the ribbon and tie a bow at the top.

KISSING BALLS

Gaily trimmed with ribbons and mistletoe, kissing balls gave proper Victorians an excuse for a Christmas kiss. These two lovely examples, while reminiscent of the classic design, have been cleverly updated.

The burgundy-flowered kissing ball is constructed from two wire bird's nests, which have been sprayed with gold paint and then wired together. It is then trimmed with handmade silk-ribbon flowers. Inside the ball, a little bird rests on silk pine sprigs. The other example, trimmed in pink-ribbon flowers, uses a Styrofoam™ ball as its base. Broken terra-cotta flowerpot pieces are hot-glued to the form. Gaps between the pieces are filled with floral moss. See detailed project directions on pages 216-217. Materials to make these balls can be purchased at florist's and craft stores.

BIRD-IN-NEST KISSING BALL

MATERIALS AND EQUIPMENT

· Metallic gold spray paint · 2 wire bird nests, 6 inches diameter · Bird, 2½ inches · Fine wire ·
· Buckram fabric, 2½ inches x 7 inches · 10 Silk pine tree sprigs · ¼ yard Burgundy wire-edged ribbon,
½ inch wide · 1⅔ yards Burgundy ribbon, ⅝ inch to 1½ inches wide ·
· 1 yard Burgundy ribbon, ⅝ inch wide · ½ yard Burgundy ribbon, ⅝ inch wide ·
· 1¼ yard Green ribbon, ⅝ inch to 1½ inches · Crinoline fabric, 4 inches x 4 inches ·
· Metallic gold beads, 3 mm · Beading thread · Dried baby's breath · Flower stamens ·
· Glue gun with glue sticks · Needle · Needle-nose pliers · Ruler · Pencil · Scissors · Wire cutters ·

DIRECTIONS

1. Use metallic gold spray paint to spray the wire nests. Let dry.

2. Use fine wire to twist three silk pine sprigs together to form a Y.

3. Measure the diameter of the wire nests. Wire the pine sprigs to the bottom edge of the smaller nest (Illustration A). Wire or hot-glue the bird to the center of the Y (Illustration B).

4. Press the wire nests together (with the bird and pine sprigs inside) so that they overlap. Shape into a ball and secure the nests with wire.

5. From the 1⅔-yard length of ribbon, cut a dozen 3½-inch pieces and seven 2½-inch pieces. To make petals, fold and hot-glue all the ribbon pieces per diagram on the next page, and pinch the ends together when the glue is cool enough to handle. Cut off the tails.

6. Use a pencil to draw a 2-inch circle on the buckram. Mark the circle at the 12, 2, 4, 6, 8, and 10 o'clock positions. Hot-glue one large petal on each mark. Then hot-glue one large petal at the 1, 3, 5, 7, 9, and 11 o'clock positions. Hot-glue seven small petals just inside the second row.

7. From the 1-yard length of ribbon, cut a dozen 2½-inch pieces. Repeat steps 5 and 6 to make and place large flower petals.

8. From the ½-yard length of ribbon, cut six 2½-inch pieces. Repeat step 5 to make petals. Mark the circle as in step 6, and hot-glue the petals to the even-numbered marks.

9. Cut the green ribbon into eleven 3½-inch pieces. Fold and hot-glue as for the petals. Hot-glue seven leaves to the back of the large flower in a semicircle. Hot-glue three leaves to the back of the medium flower at the 5, 9, and 11 o'clock positions. Hot-glue the remaining leaf to the back of the small flower.

10. Draw three circles on the crinoline to fit the flower centers. Using needle and thread, sew the gold beads onto the fabric to fill the circles. Carefully cut around the beaded circles. Hot-glue the circles into the center of each flower.

11. Make a hanging loop from the wired ribbon by threading it through the top of the ball. Knot the ribbon. Pull the knot down toward the ball and hot-glue in place.

12. Hot-glue the pine sprigs, stamens, and baby's breath to the top of the ball. Hot-glue the large flower to one side of the top of the ball. Hot-glue the medium and small flowers to the top and opposite side of the ball.

A. Attach silk pine sprigs to the edge of the nest using wire.

B. Attach bird to the pine sprigs using hot glue.

TERRA-COTTA KISSING BALL

MATERIALS AND EQUIPMENT

· Terra-cotta flowerpot, 5 inches diameter · Styrofoam™ ball, 5 inches diameter · Green floral moss ·
· 1 yard Satin cording, 3 mm · 5 Large velvet leaves · Pastel velvet rose leaves ·
· Buckram fabric, 2½ inches x 7 inches · 10 Silk pine tree sprigs ·
· 1⅔ yards Pink ribbon, ⅝ inch to 1½ inches wide · 1 yard Pink ribbon, ⅝ inch wide ·
· ½ yard Pink ribbon, ⅝ inch wide · 1¼ yard Green ribbon, ⅝ inch to 1½ inches wide ·
· 1 yard Pink wire-edged ribbon, ¾ inch · Crinoline fabric, 4 inches x 4 inches · Metallic gold beads, 3 mm ·
· Beading thread · Dried baby's breath · Flower stamens · Glue gun with glue sticks ·
· Hammer · Pencil · Needle · Scissors ·

C. Apply hot glue to the terra-cotta pieces and arrange them on Styrofoam ball.

D. Apply hot glue between the terra-cotta pieces on Styrofoam ball and attach the green floral moss.

DIRECTIONS

1. Place the flowerpot inside a folded newspaper. Using a hammer, break the pot into pieces, 2 inches x 1 inch. Apply hot glue to the terra-cotta pieces and arrange them on the Styrofoam ball, leaving ½-inch to ¾-inch gaps (Illustration C). Apply hot glue to the gaps on the Styrofoam ball and attach the green floral moss until all the gaps are covered (Illustration D).

2. To form a loop for hanging, fold the cording in half twice. Tie a knot in the folded end. Hot-glue the loose ends together. Using a pencil, poke a hole in the top of the ball. Hot-glue the loose ends into the hole.

3. Starting at the top of the ball, hot-glue three large velvet leaves down one side of the ball. Repeat using two leaves on the opposite side. Hot-glue the pastel rose leaves on the front of the ball.

4. Repeat steps 5-10 from *Bird-in-Nest Kissing Ball*, opposite page.

5. Hot-glue the large flower to one side on the top of the ball. Hot-glue the medium and small flowers on the top opposite side of the ball.

6. Using the wire-edged ribbon, make a six-loop bow and hot-glue it to the top of the ball. Hot-glue bunches of baby's breath and stamens underneath the leaves.

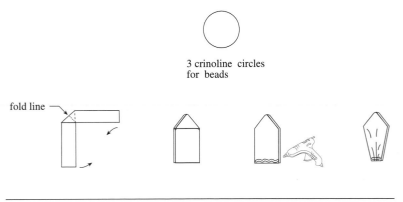

3 crinoline circles
for beads

fold line

SPICY FRUIT POMANDERS

Originally small filigree balls of gold, silver, or ivory filled with fragrant spices and an ambergris fixative, pomanders (from the French *pomme d'ambre,* or apple of ambergris) were used as early as the Middle Ages, when they were worn to ward off unpleasant odors. Today's version of the pomander is made by studding a piece of fruit with cloves and curing it in a mixture of ground spices with orrisroot as a fixative.

Pomanders are lovely holiday gifts.

Not only do they make fragrant decorations that can be hung from ribbons or arranged in bowls, but when placed in closets, they help keep woolens moth-free.

A pomander's scent usually lasts for several years, but can be refreshed by dipping the pomander in warm water, then rolling it in fresh spices to which a drop or two of cinnamon or clove oil has been added. Leave the pomander in the mixture for a few days, then use as before.

MATERIALS AND EQUIPMENT

· 6 to 8 assorted firm, thin-skinned apples, oranges, lemons, and limes ·
· ½ pound whole, large-headed cloves with strong scent ·
· ¼ cup ground cinnamon · ¼ cup ground cloves ·
· 2 tablespoons ground nutmeg ·
· 2 tablespoons ground allspice · ¼ cup powdered orrisroot ·
· Nut pick or slender knitting needle for piercing fruit (optional) ·
· Ribbon (optional) · Small paintbrush ·

◆

ASSEMBLY

1. Hold a piece of the fruit firmly, without squeezing. Insert the cloves at ⅛- to ¼-inch intervals in rows (or at random) over the surface; the fruit will shrink as it dries, closing up the spaces. (If you have difficulty inserting the cloves, you can pierce the fruit first with the point of a nut pick or knitting needle, but take care to keep the holes small or the cloves will fall out when the fruit dries.) If you intend to hang your pomanders from ribbons, you can leave a 1-inch "path" around the fruit to provide a channel to keep the ribbon in place.

2. Blend the spices and orrisroot in a small bowl. One at a time, roll each piece of fruit in the mixture, coating it generously to keep air out. (Any pomander you start should be completed to this point within twenty-four hours to eliminate the possibility of mold forming.)

3. Place the spice-coated fruit in a large bowl, cover with the spice mixture, and set in a warm, dry place to dry. Turn the fruit daily, making sure the spices are evenly distributed. Drying can take from two weeks to a month, depending on the size of the fruit. The pomanders will be hard when they are completely dry.

4. Remove the pomanders from the spice mixture and dust off the excess with the brush. Tie with ribbon, if desired.

Pine Cone Christmas Tree

Extend the joy of the season throughout the house with pretty pine cone trees. This tabletop Christmas tree can be made in a variety of sizes or colors and trimmed. Use moss, dried flowers, greenery, ribbons, crackle-painted ornaments—even wrapped candy. The clear garland on the gingham ribbon-trimmed tree is created with glue sticks and a glue gun. Colored or sparkle glue sticks can be substituted for a different effect.

A. Tear copper leaf into small pieces and apply with old paintbrush.

MATERIALS AND EQUIPMENT

· Styrofoam™ cone, 13 inches tall ·
· Chicken wire, 22 inches x 13 inches ·
· Pine cones, about 2 inches long · Gold-leaf adhesive ·
· Copper leafing · Patina-aging solution, rust ·
· 14 wooden beads, ³/₈ inch diameter ·
· Wooden finial, 2¹/₂ inches tall ·
· Green, red, and off-white acrylic paint · Crackle medium ·
· Green floral moss · Pepper berries ·
· 1 yard wire-edged ribbon, ⁵/₈ inch wide · Wire, 24 gauge ·
· Glue gun with glue sticks · Needle-nose pliers ·
· Wire cutters · Paintbrushes ·

◆

B. Spray copper leafing with Patina aging solution for yellow and green color effect.

DIRECTIONS

1. Using a paintbrush, apply the gold-leaf adhesive on the inside edges of the pine cones. Tear the copper leafing into small pieces. Using a paintbrush, apply the copper leafing on the inside edges of the pine cones (Illustration A). Apply the rust patina over the copper leafing (Illustration B). Set aside until the copper leafing turns yellow and green. Or, using a glue gun, slowly drape the glue around the pine cones to create a frosted effect (Illustrations C and D).

2. Roll the chicken wire around the Styrofoam™ cone and secure the edges together using wire.

3. Wrap wire around the center of each pine cone and secure each to the chicken wire. Repeat until the cone is covered.

4. Using the off-white paint, paint the wooden beads. Using the red and green paints, paint the finial as desired. Set aside to dry.

5. Using the crackle medium, generously paint the beads and the finial. Set aside for two to four hours until thoroughly dry.

6. Using the red paint, paint the surface of seven beads. Using the green paint, paint the surface of the remaining beads.

7. Using the red and green paints, paint red over red and green over green on the finial. Using the off-white paint, wash the surface of the finial to accent the crackle effect.

8. Hot-glue the moss and pepper berries to fill any open spaces.

9. Make bows from the ribbon, arrange and hot glue in place.

10. Hot-glue the wooden beads to the tree as desired.

C. For a frosted effect, apply the glue slowly, allowing it to drape in threads.

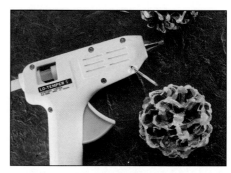

D. Hot glue will set up as it cools creating a lasting garland.

CHRISTMAS STOCKINGS

No Christmas would be complete without Christmas stockings. While the classic custom is to hang them by the fireplace, stockings can decorate trees, garlands, wreaths, shelves, or any part of the home that needs a touch of holiday cheer. These decorative Christmas stockings are made from felt and stitched by hand with contrasting embroidery floss. Appliqué designs add interest and color to the basic stocking. Using self-stick fusible webbing, applying the appliqués is simple. Felt and floss colors can be personalized to match any decorating scheme. Fill stockings with candy canes, other seasonal sweets, or tiny gifts.

MATERIALS AND EQUIPMENT

· Black, blue, brown, dark blue, green, gold, and red felt,
8¹⁄₂ inches x 11 inches each · Tracing paper · Pencil ·
· Fusible webbing · Black and white embroidery floss ·
· Glue gun with glue sticks ·
· Iron and ironing board · Needle · Scissors ·

◆

DIRECTIONS

1. Trace or photocopy the stocking pattern on pages 224 and 225 at 100%. Use the pattern to cut two pieces of felt for each stocking.

2. Trace all the appliqué patterns except the bow on the paper side of the fusible webbing. Using an iron, fuse the webbing to the felt according to the manufacturer's directions. Cut out the felt appliqué pieces.

3. Arrange the appliqués on the stockings and fuse them in place.

4. Using blanket stitch, sew around the appliqués. Using black embroidery floss, stitch French knots for the snowman's eyes. Align the stocking pieces together and blanket-stitch the edges, except the top.

5. Cut the bow from the green felt. Take one side of the bow in each hand and twist. Hot-glue the center of the bow on the top gift pictured on pattern.

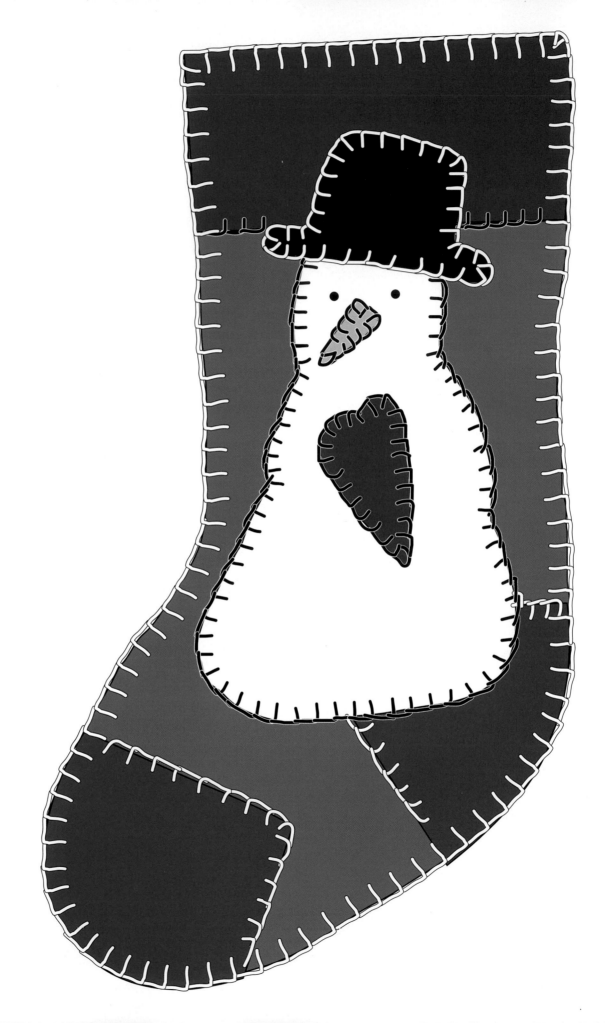

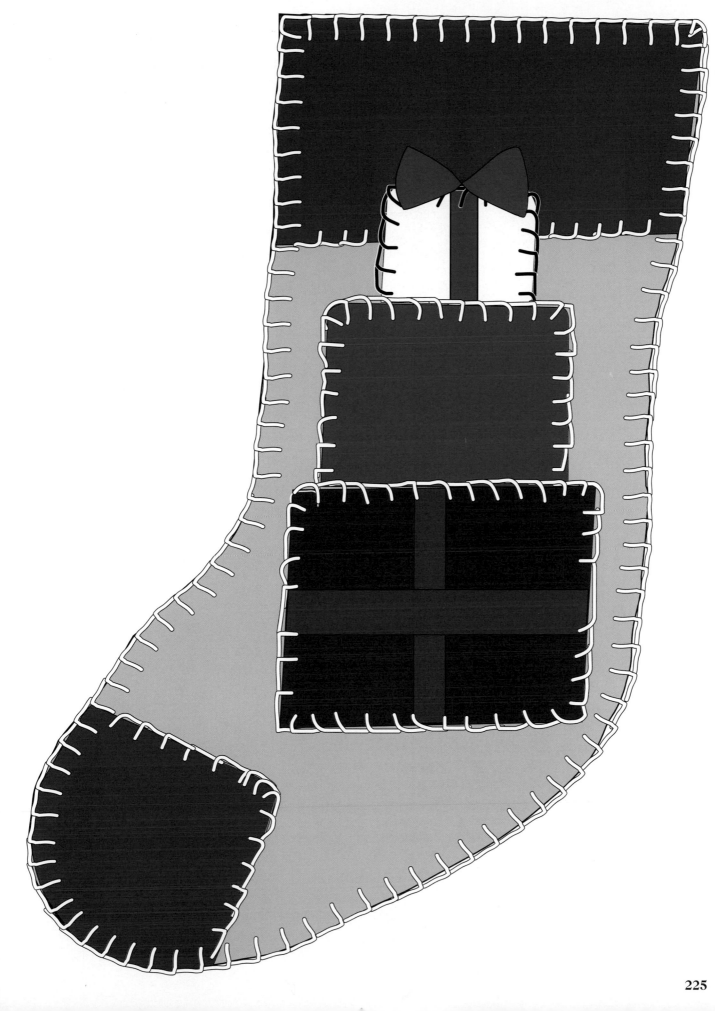

STAMPED GLASS ORNAMENTS

Handmade glass holiday ornaments are a great way to decorate the holiday tree. These ornaments feature stamped artwork, but any kind of artwork or family photographs can be used. Artwork trimmed from greeting cards or wrapping paper, or found on decorative stickers, can be used to accent these glass ornaments. Photographs can even be incorporated in ornament designs to make each ornament a personal keepsake. When making these ornaments, be certain to start with precision-cut glass. Professional glass cutting is recommended. Pieces should line up perfectly to make soldering easier. Cover your work surface to prevent possible damage. When covering glass edges with copper foil tape, make certain not to overlap the tape. A little solder goes a long way. If this is the first time using a soldering iron, consider practicing on a scrap piece of glass first. The soldering iron must be hot to work efficiently. Stamping supplies and handmade papers are available at most craft and stationery stores. Soldering supplies can be found in plumbing supply or hardware stores. Copper foil tape and cut glass can be purchased through a stained glass store.

MATERIALS AND EQUIPMENT

· Green handmade paper, 4 inches x 6 inches (heavyweight) ·

· Red handmade paper, 2 inches x 3 inches (heavyweight) · White handmade paper (lightweight) ·

· Angel stamp, 1³/₄ inches tall · Merry Christmas stamp, 1³/₄ inches long · Christmas tree stamp, 1³/₄ inches tall · Santa stamp, 1³/₄ inches tall · Snowflake stamp, ¹/₂ inch ·

· 3 Star stamps, ¹/₄ inch, ¹/₂ inch, 1 inch · 2 Evergreen stamps, 1¹/₂ inches, 2 inches tall ·

· Black, clear gold, green, and silver pigment ink pads · Clear, gold, and white embossing powder ·

· Clear embossing pen · Set of felt brush-tip pens · Set of watercolors ·

· Decoupage glue · Glue stick · Silver-backed copper foil tape · 10 Pieces glass, 2 inches x 3 inches ·

· Paper clips · All-purpose flux · Patina for soldering · Soldering iron and solder, 60/40 ·

· Ribbon, ¹/₄ inch wide · Craft knife · Decorative edge scissors · Heat gun ·

· Paintbrushes · Scissors · Toothpicks · Wire cutters ·

DIRECTIONS

Angel

1. Stamp angel using black ink on white handmade paper and sprinkle with clear embossing powder. Set powder with heat gun.
2. Fill in angel wings and horn using clear embossing pen and sprinkle with gold embossing powder. Set powder with heat gun.
3. Using color felt-tip pens, color angel's body and banner.
4. Using watercolors, paint body and face.
5. Using water and paintbrush, moisten around outside edge of stamped angel. Use a craft knife to carefully tear away excess paper.
6. Using glue stick, glue angel to 2-inch x 3-inch piece of green handmade paper.
7. Repeat steps 1 to 4 and glue on opposite side of green handmade paper.

Christmas Tree

1. Using color felt-tip pens, color directly onto Christmas tree stamp using desired colors.
2. Stamp tree on white handmade paper.
3. Using water and paintbrush, moisten around outside edge of stamped tree. Use a toothpick to feather edges and tear away excess paper.
4. Moisten and tear feathered edge from green handmade paper slightly larger than tree. Using glue stick, glue tree to green paper.
5. Repeat steps 1 to 3 and glue on opposite side of green handmade paper.

Santa/Merry Christmas

1. Stamp Santa using black ink on white handmade paper. Emboss using clear embossing powder. Set powder with the heat gun.
2. Fill in fur trim and ball using clear embossing pen and sprinkle with clear embossing powder. Set powder with the heat gun.
3. Using watercolors, color Santa's face and beard.
4. Cut Santa image out.
5. Using decorative scissors, cut a 1⅞-inch x 2⅞-inch rectangle from red handmade paper. Using glue stick, glue Santa to upper half of paper.
6. Stamp "Merry Christmas" using silver ink on bottom half of red handmade paper. Emboss using clear embossing powder. Set powder using heat gun.
7. Repeat steps 1 to 4 and glue on opposite side of red handmade paper. Repeat step 6.

Stars on Glass

1. Stamp multiple sizes of stars on two 2-inch x 3-inch pieces of glass using silver and gold ink. Emboss

using clear embossing powder. Set powder using heat gun. Note: Embossing powder will take longer to melt on glass. Glass will become very hot. Allow glass to cool completely before handling or placing glass pieces together.
2. Place stamped sides together for final assembly.

Evergreen Trees

1. Stamp large tree using green ink on the white handmade paper.
2. Stamp small tree using green ink on a scrap piece of paper to remove some ink. Stamp small tree slightly overlapping larger tree. The small tree will look faded.
3. Cut out the trees. Turn the trees over and repeat steps 1 to 2.
4. Arrange trees between two pieces of 2-inch x 3-inch glass. Determine where other trees and snowflakes will be stamped.
5. Remove cutout trees, stamp trees using green ink on glass pieces. Emboss using clear embossing powder.
6. Stamp snowflakes using clear ink on glass pieces. Emboss using white embossing powder. Set embossing powder with heat gun. See note on step 1 of Stars on Glass.
7. Using decoupage glue, glue cutout trees to stamped side of glass. Place stamped sides of glass together for assembly.

Ornament Assembly

1. Sandwich artwork between two pieces of glass.
2. Using copper foil tape, tape around the four sides of the glass pieces, making sure that tape overlaps both pieces of glass on each side.
3. Use an old paintbrush to lightly brush flux on foil. Note: If flux is too heavy it will penetrate between glass pieces.
4. Heat up solder iron. Holding solder wire in one hand and solder iron in the other, solder tape over glass, working as carefully and quickly as possible. Beads or pools may form, giving the ornament an antique look.
5. Use wire cutters to cut paper clip, leaving a horseshoe shape for hanger. Lay paper clip on the top of the soldered edge. Using soldering iron, solder a bead of solder over the paper clip. After cooling, cut a length of ribbon and tie through ornament holder to hang.
6. Clean glass using soap and slightly damp cloth. Do not use running water to clean; water may leak in, damaging artwork.
7. Brush a light amount of patina on soldered area, following manufacturer's instructions. Repeat if more color is desired.

GARLAND IDEAS

Creating Christmas garlands like those at right, which display some innovative twists on more familiar themes, can be as much fun for adults as it is for children. And making them is a simple matter of using ordinary materials in imaginative ways. Most of those shown here—beads, pretzels, macaroni, gumdrops, tiny bells, cork balls, and stick-on stars—are available at novelty stores and supermarkets. For the best results when making and storing garlands, consider the following tips:

◆ If you want to string materials on an "invisible" thread, use sturdy nylon or buttonhole thread.

◆ If you want your "string" to show, use colorful ribbons or thick, shiny cords.

◆ To string tiny pinecones, which are fragile, lay them on a tabletop and pierce them gently with a sharp sewing needle threaded with nylon or buttonhole thread.

◆ If you wish to spray-paint any of the materials—paint works particularly well on pasta and pinecones—be sure to do so before stringing them.

◆ To store your garlands tangle-free, carefully wind them around cardboard wrapping-paper tubes.

MAKING CORNUCOPIAS

Filled with popcorn, candy, fruit, or nuts, paper cornucopias like those above once found a popular place on the Christmas tree. Directions for making these small containers appeared in late-19th-century ladies' magazines. At that time, candy and "sweetmeats" played an important holiday role; these inexpensive gifts were eagerly awaited by children, who were seldom given the opportunity to feast on such treats during the rest of the year.

Cornucopias still make festive ornaments and are easy to craft. You will need lightweight cardboard for a pattern, decorative papers (wrapping paper is fine), trims (try stickers, braid, sequins, and fancy ribbons), craft glue, spray adhesive, a drafting compass, and scissors.

Begin by using the compass to draft a quarter-circle pattern onto lightweight cardboard (the cornucopias shown here have a radius of 4, 5, or 6 inches). On one straight edge of the pattern add a ¼-inch-wide overlap allowance, then taper the allowance at the point; cut the pattern out.

For each cornucopia, trace the pattern onto a piece of decorative paper and cut to make the outside piece; then reverse the pattern and repeat to make a lining. On the wrong sides, spray the paper pieces with adhesive and stick them together. Apply the craft glue to the allowance on the outside paper, then roll the paper into a cone. Trim as desired. Glue a piece of ribbon to the inside rim for a handle and cover the ends with a band of trim.

CHRISTMAS CANDLE CHIMNEYS

Use these Christmas candle chimneys individually to add the soft glow of candlelight to your holiday decor, or group them among a few boughs of pine and holly to create a beautiful tabletop centerpiece. While the results are striking, decorating the hurricane chimneys is surprisingly simple. Trace or photocopy the provided patterns and place them inside the chimney, then paint the outside of the shade with enamel glass paints, following the pattern. Borders can be painted on either the top or bottom of the chimneys. Enamel glass paints come in both air-dry and oven-cure varieties.

Candle chimneys are wonderful decorative accessories any time of the year. Design your own pattern by tracing favorite motifs onto paper and then painting the design in colors appropriate to the season.

MATERIALS AND EQUIPMENT

· Glass hurricane chimneys · Tracing paper · Pencil · Black, green, red, white, and yellow enamel glass paints · · Paintbrush · Masking tape · Dishwashing liquid ·

◆

DIRECTIONS

1. Wash the glass chimneys with dishwashing liquid and water. Sticker glue can be removed with steel wool, if necessary.

2. Create your own pattern or simply trace or color photocopy the pattern on the next page (sized for a medium chimney). Tape the pattern to the inside of the chimney, cutting the border and the center design patterns into separate pieces if needed to fit the curvature of the glass (Illustration A).

3. Paint the design on the chimney, rotating the pattern around the chimney (Illustration B). Allow each paint color to dry before proceeding. Note: See manufacturer's directions; some paints may require curing in the oven.

A. Tape the pattern to the inside of the glass chimney.

B. Paint the design on the glass. Allow each paint color to dry before proceeding.

CHRISTMAS DEER

Wrapped in bold holiday fabrics, these festive deer provide a striking woodland accent to any holiday decor. The deer are fabric-covered papier-mâché forms embellished with greenery, decorative cording, and ornaments. A plastic ornament, cut in halves and painted, is used to make the broken-ornament nest. Other birds are housed in the ornament birdhouses hanging from the plaid deer's antlers. Crackle-painted birds perch on both deer amid moss and floral accents.

MATERIALS AND EQUIPMENT

· 2 Papier-mâché deer, 1 lying, 1 standing · Christmas cotton fabric, 2 yards · Cording or embroidery floss ·
· 2 Round plastic ornaments, 3 inches diameter · Round plastic ornament, 2½ inches diameter ·
· Plastic teardrop ornament, 3 inches · 3 Wooden eggs, 1 inch long · 5 Carved wooden birds, 2¼ inches long ·
· Blue, dark brown, dark green, light tan, off-white, and red acrylic paints · Crackle medium ·
· Antique medium, warm brown · Spray sealer · Brass ornament hangers · 4 Douglas fir sprays ·
· Grapevine wreath, 3 inches diameter · Bay leaves · Mixed nuts in shell · Pepper berries · Raffia ·
· Small pine cones · Styrofoam™, 2 inches x 1 inch · Spray adhesive · Glue gun with glue sticks ·
· Industrial-strength glue · Craft glue · Cheesecloth · Old toothbrush · Tin snips ·

◆

DIRECTIONS

1. Tear the fabric into strips 1 inch by 2 inches. Using the craft glue, glue one end of a strip to one end of a deer. Wrap the strip around the deer, overlapping the edges. Secure the end with craft glue. Continue applying strips to the deer until each is completely covered.

2. Cut a long length of cording or floss and wrap randomly around the deer, securing both ends with craft glue.

3. Using tin snips, cut a jagged edge around one of the 3-inch round ornaments, creating two halves.

4. Spray the plastic ornaments with adhesive so the paint will adhere. Let dry.

5. Paint one round ornament and the cut ornaments with red paint. Paint the teardrop ornament dark green. Mix equal parts of the off-white and light tan paint; paint the eggs and remaining ornament. Paint a base coat on the birds with blue paint. Paint a circle on the whole ornaments with dark brown paint for a bird entrance.

6. Dip the old toothbrush into the light tan paint. Practice splatter painting first on scrap paper. Use your forefinger or a toothpick to push the bristles toward you; as bristles spring back into position, they will splatter tan specks onto the paper. Splatter paint the eggs.

7. Using the crackle medium, generously paint the birds. Set aside for two to four hours. Paint the entire surface of the birds with the off-white paint. As the paint dries, cracks will appear. Float the light blue paint around the outside edges of the birds. Using the antique medium, paint the surface of the birds. Using a piece of cheesecloth, wipe off excess antique medium. Spray all the painted surfaces with spray sealer.

8. Using industrial-strength glue, glue one half of the cut ornament just inside the other half.

9. Hot-glue the brass hangers to the tops of the ornaments. Hot-glue the ornament to lying reindeer's back. Hot-glue the piece of Styrofoam™ inside. Hot-glue moss to cover the Styrofoam™. Hot-glue the eggs in place on the moss.

10. Arrange two Douglas fir sprays around the ornament and hot-glue in place. Arrange the bay leaves, nuts, pepper berries, pine cones, raffia, and one bird on the fir spray and hot-glue in place. Arrange the moss, small raffia bow, and a bird on the wreath and hot-glue in place. Hang or hot-glue the wreath on an antler. Hot-glue the moss and one bird to the inside of the other antler.

11. Arrange two Douglas Fir sprays around the back of the standing deer's neck and hot-glue in place. Arrange the bay leaves, nuts, pepper berries, pine cones, and raffia on the pine spray and hot-glue in place.

12. Arrange the moss, pine cones, bay leaves, and pepper berries around the bird entrance on the ornaments and hot-glue in place. Thread a strand of raffia through each ornament holder and tie to the antlers. Hot-glue one bird to the bird entrance on an ornament. Hot-glue the moss and remaining bird above the deer's ear.

CHRISTMAS SACHETS

These delightfully whimsical sachets can be used as colorful trim for packages, trees, and garlands or as fragrant accessories in any part of the home. Fill the sachets with purchased or homemade potpourri. Dried rose petals, mint leaves, and cloves can be combined with a few drops of essential oil for an aromatic potpourri. Select fabric in colors and patterns to complement home decor, tree decorations, or gift wrap. Materials to make these sachets are available at fabric and craft stores.

MATERIALS AND EQUIPMENT

· Sachet patterns (opposite page) · Gold and red felt squares · Red plaid cotton fabric, ⅛ yard ·
· Gold print cotton fabric, ⅛ yard · Light green stripe cotton fabric, ⅛ yard ·
· Fusible webbing, ¹/₁₂ yard · Black, gold, green, and red embroidery floss ·
· Potpourri · 16-gauge Wire, 10 inches · 20-gauge Wire, 8 inches ·
· Craft glue · Iron and ironing board • Needle · Needle-nose pliers · Scissors ·

◆

DIRECTIONS

1. Trace or photocopy the sachet patterns. Using the red felt, cut out one bird body. Using the gold felt, cut out one cat body with wings.

2. Trace the bird body onto the paper side of the fusible webbing. Using an iron, fuse the webbing to the red plaid cotton fabric according to the manufacturer's directions. Trace the beak and wings onto the paper side of the webbing; fuse to the gold print cotton fabric. Trace the cat body and paws onto the paper side of the webbing; fuse to the light green stripe fabric. Cut out the pieces.

4. Arrange the beak on the bird body and fuse it in place. Arrange the paws on the cat body and fuse them in place. Arrange the wings on the back of the striped cat body (allow ¼ inch overlap) and fuse them in place.

5. Using the black floss, sew French knots for the eyes. Using the red floss, embroider the cat's nose and sew French knots for the holly berries. Follow the stitching diagram to embroider the holly leaves with the green floss.

6. Match the felt backs to the cotton fronts. Using blanket stitches, sew around the sachets, leaving a small opening for the potpourri.

7. Fill the sachets with the potpourri. Finish blanket-stitching the sachets closed.

8. Use needle-nose pliers to bend 20-gauge wire into a halo for the cat. Place craft glue on the end of the halo and insert between the fabric layers.

9. Use needle-nose pliers to bend the 16-gauge wire into bird-feet shapes. Place craft glue on the ends of the legs and insert between the fabric layers.

stitch guide

STAMPED HOLIDAY TRAY

Present Santa with holiday treats set out on this colorful, easy-to-make tray accented with rubber-stamp artwork. Stamps are fun and simple to use, and they are available in thousands of designs. The purchased tray is first painted and then embellished with a variety of stamped images. Finally, resin, which adds a thick, plastic-like coating to flat objects, is used to seal the decorated surface of the tray. The resin is poured and smoothed over the surface, then heated with a small propane torch so it will harden. If desired, the tray can be sealed with an acrylic spray sealer instead of resin. Materials for this project are available at craft, stationery, and hardware stores.

MATERIALS AND EQUIPMENT

· Wooden tray, 16 inches x 20 inches ·
· Dark green, ivory, light purple, light tan, mauve, metallic gold, olive green, pink, and yellow acrylic paints · White paint pen ·
· Assorted holiday stamps, ranging in sizes $\frac{1}{4}$ inch to $3\frac{3}{4}$ inches ·
· Black, brown, light green, red, and violet pigment ink pads ·
· Clear, burgundy, and gold embossing powder ·
· Clear embossing pen · Acrylic spray sealer · Resin ·
· Wooden tongue depressor · Cardboard box · Heat gun ·
· Paintbrushes · Propane torch ·

◆

DIRECTIONS

1. Leaving a $\frac{1}{2}$-inch border along the outside edge, divide the tray surface into various-sized rectangles and squares similar to quilt blocks. Keep the sizes of the holiday stamps in mind.

2. Paint the sides of the tray with dark green acrylic paint. Paint a $\frac{1}{2}$-inch border using half mauve and half ivory acrylic paint. Paint each block a different color, mixing colors as desired.

3. Stamp each block with the desired ink and stamps. Emboss the designs with embossing powders. Color with the white paint pen and acrylic paints as desired.

4. Draw "stitched" lines between the blocks, using a clear embossing pen, then sprinkle with gold embossing powder. Set the powder with the heat gun. Try different stitches for variety.

5. Use the acrylic spray sealer to seal the tray surface. If sealing the surface with acrylic sealer rather than resin, apply six to seven coats of sealer.

6. Prepare the resin according to the manufacturer's directions. Pour over the decorated surface of the tray and smooth it, using a wooden tongue depressor.

7. Using the propane torch carefully, release the resin gases by moving the torch side to side 6 inches from the surface. Follow the manufacturer's directions as to the number of times the resin should be heated with the torch.

8. To protect the tray from dust as the resin sets, cover it with a cardboard box. Set aside 24 to 36 hours, or until the resin is hard.

CHRISTMAS HATBOXES

Fabric-covered boxes can be just as delightful as and often more practical than any gift they may contain. They can also do double duty as decorative accessories while providing storage. Plain cardboard hatboxes are covered with decorative holiday fabrics and then accented with an assortment of fabric ap pliqué designs. Self-stick fusible webbing makes this project much easier than it appears. Although the appliqué looks hand-stitched, no sewing is required. The "stitches" around the appliqué designs are applied with a fine-point permanent pen. Hatboxes can be purchased at most craft stores.

MATERIALS AND EQUIPMENT

· Cardboard hatbox, 7 inches diameter x 3 inches tall ·
· Cardboard hatbox, 7³/₄ inches diameter x 4 inches tall ·
· Cardboard hatbox, 10¹/₄ inches diameter x 6 inches tall ·
· Cardboard hatbox, 12³/₄ inches diameter x 7¹/₂ inches tall ·
· Fusible webbing, 4¹/₂ yards · Assorted 45-inch-wide Christmas color fabrics,
1 yard per hatbox · 45-inch-wide fabric, ¹/₄ yard each: blue, brown, black, gold,
green, pink, red, and white · Black permanent fine-point pen ·
· Fabric tape measure · Iron and ironing board · Scissors ·

◆

DIRECTIONS

1. For the hatbox, measure its circumference, adding an extra 1¹/₂ inches, then measure its depth, adding an extra 2 inches. Cut the fusible webbing to the measurements.

2. Using an iron, fuse the webbing to the fabric (follow the manufacturer's directions). Cut the fabric around the fusible webbing edges. Fuse the fabric to the side of the box, overlapping the fabric ends and allowing a 1-inch overlap on the top and bottom.

3. Use scissors to clip the edges of the fabric to the rims of the box at 1-inch intervals. Fold the fabric over and fuse it to the inside and the bottom of the box.

4. For the box lid, trace around the lid on the paper side of the fusible webbing, adding an extra 1 inch. For the finishing strip, measure the circumference of the lid, adding an extra 1¹/₂ inches, then measure the depth of the lid, adding an extra 1 inch. Cut the two webbing pieces to the measurements. Fuse them to the fabric and cut out.

5. Fuse the fabric to the box lid (refer to step 2).

6. Repeat steps 1-5 for each box.

7. Photocopy the appliqué patterns on pages 242-245. Note: Photocopy at percentages shown under pattern. Trace onto the paper side of the fusible webbing. Fuse the webbing to the fabric. Cut out the appliqué pieces.

8. Arrange the appliqués on the boxes and fuse them into place.

9. Use a fine-point permanent pen to mark blanket stitches around the appliqué edges. Mark the faces of the angels and Santa.

Trace or photocopy at 100%.

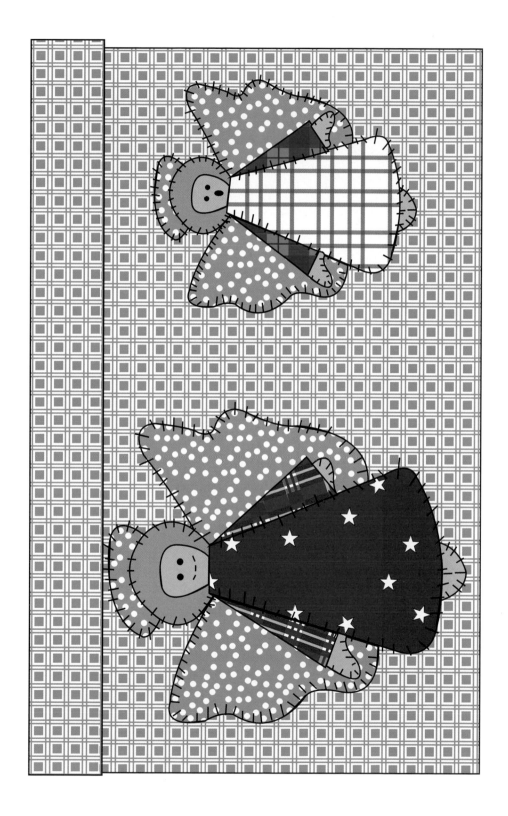

Trace or photocopy at 100%.

Photocopy at 136%.

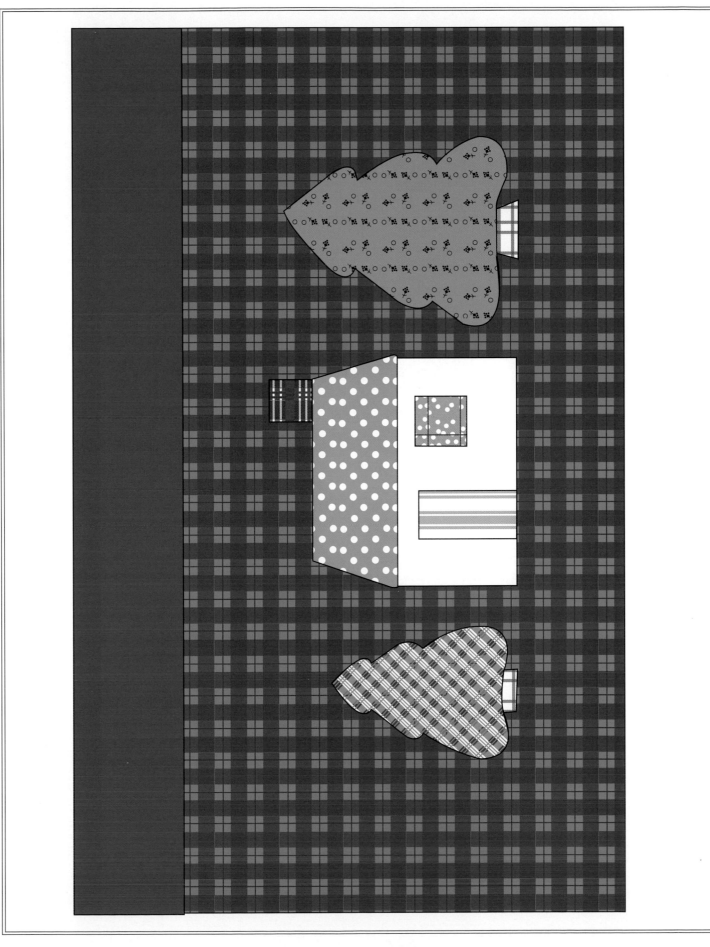

Photocopy at 136%.

ROMANTIC GIFT WRAPS

Everyone appreciates a surprise at Christmas, and special gift wraps add to the pleasure. The well-dressed packages here and on the following pages will give you some imaginative ideas for wrappings that will be as memorable as your gifts.

The packages at right convey a romantic, old-fashioned feeling. Papers, fabrics, ribbons, and trims for wrapping presents like these can come from many different sources, such as art supply, decorating, and fabric shops. For a particularly rich look, try overwrapping gifts with two layers of paper or fabric. A sheet of lacy rice paper or a piece of sheer organdy or tulle is effective over dark-toned metallic paper. Or, use a narrow wallpaper border as an elegant trim on contrasting, solid-color paper.

Devoting some thought to the gift-recipient's hobbies and interests will help you make creative use of your supplies. A bouquet of dried roses, for instance, is the perfect trim for a flower-lover's present. An artist or craftsperson might appreciate a package done up in handmade marbleized paper, while wallpaper makes an appropriate wrap for a gift to someone who is redecorating.

The dressed-up packages at right are almost too pretty to open. On some, the tops and bottoms are wrapped separately so that the decorated boxes can be reused.

CASUAL GIFT WRAPS

The casual gift wrappings at left, most of which are created from paper and other supplies that might be found around the house, make great family projects. Ordinary craft and construction papers, for example, are easily transformed into Christmas wrappings with sponge printing. Simply cut clean, dry sponges into various shapes with sharp scissors, or use a firm apple or pear sliced in half. Daub the sponge or fruit in acrylic paint and print.

Large envelopes can be dressed up with stickers and ribbons, and paper bags make convenient wrappings for cookies and other Christmas baked goods. Use rubber stamps to decorate the bags with repeat patterns. Or, cut the tops of the bags into scalloped borders and embellish them with paper-punch designs. You can then make a row of paper-punch holes or small slits and weave ribbon, raffia, or yarn through the openings.

Some wraps might also be part of the gift. Linen towels secured with ribbon, for example, make lively— and useful—packages. And for a small gift, a handmade fabric bag with a drawstring tie is a good alternative to a box; the bag can then be filled with potpourri and reused by the recipient as a sachet.

The fabric scraps, paper bags, envelopes, and other household items at left are trimmed with decorative stickers and ribbons to create innovative Christmas wrappings.

Photography Credits

Arizona Photographic Associates: page 23 (bottom left)

Culver Pictures: page 22 (bottom right), 23 (bottom right)

Kevin Dilley: pages 202-204, 210-211, 214-217, 220-223, 226, 232, 234, 236, 238-240

Free Library of Philadelphia: page 23 (top right)

The Henry Francis duPont Winterhur Museum: page 22 (top right)

Christopher Lawrence: pages 170-171, 177-179, 182, 186-187, 194-197, 200

The Library of Congress: page 96 (far left)

David Lund, courtesy of Houston Metropolitan Magazine: pages 42-47

Michael Luppino: page 90 (left)

Steven Mays: frontispiece, pages 10-21, 50-55, 68-75, 78-82, 86 (left), 98-106, 108-109, 114-115, 118-119, 122-166, 172-173, 180-181, 184-185, 190-191, 199, 206-209, 212-213, 218-219, 230-231, 246-249

The New York Library Picture Collection: pages 22 (top left and bottom left), 23 (top left and bottom center)

George Ross: pages 8, 24-29 (except 24 left), 30-39 (except 35 right and 39 right), 48-49, 56-67, 84-89 (except 86 left), 90-95 (except 90 left, 110-113, 116-117, 120-121

Rob Whitcomb: pages 24 (left), 35 (right), 39 (right), 76 (top left and bottom center), 77 (top row)

Acknowledgments

Our thanks to Patrick Bell, Robert and Cristina Davila Brodsky, Mary Smith Carson, Abbie Chaykin, Lee Cochran, Rita Entmacher Cohen, Jimmy Cramer, Bobbie and Player Crosby, Dave DeWitt, Weldine and John Dossett, Jane and Jack Fitzpatrick, Vito Giallo, Gotham Book Mart Gallery, Susan and Jack Hale, Hallmark Cards, Edwin Hild, Marlene Johnson, Audrey and Doug Julian, Christina and Michael Kearney, Robert M. Merck, Bettie and Seymour Mintz, Judith and Dave Murtagh, Jean Palm, Sandra and James Pape, Stephanie Richardson of Myers Communicounsel, Inc., Malcolm Rogers, Cynthia Schaffner, Joel Schiff, Harold and Joyce Screen, Dee Shapiro, Philip V. Snyder, Donna and Peter Steffen, Phyllis Steiss Wetherill, Ed Weaver, William Woys Weaver, Etherl and Win Wilson, and Mark Winchester.

Microwave oven courtesy of Litton Microwave Cooking Products.
CleanTop range courtesy of the Whirlpool Corporation.

Index